The Economics of Freedom

*What Your Professors
Won't Tell You*

The Economics of Freedom

What Your Professors Won't Tell You

Selected Works of Frédéric Bastiat

Foreword by F.A. Hayek

Closing Essay by Tom G. Palmer

Students For Liberty
Jameson Books, Inc.

Published by Students For Liberty / Jameson Books, Inc.

Reprinted with the permission of the Foundation for Economic Education.
www.FEE.org

Edited by Clark Ruper
Copyediting by Hannah Mead and Charles King
Cover design by Valerie Crain
Book design by Cox-King Multimedia: www.ckmm.com
Bastiat translated by Seymour Cain

For information and other requests please write Students For Liberty, PO Box
17321, Arlington, VA 22216, or Jameson Books, Inc., 722 Columbus Street,
P.O. Box 738, Ottawa, Illinois 61350.

ISBN 978-0-89803-169-0

Printed in the United States of America

Contents

Introduction

The Economics of Freedom is a joint project of the Atlas Economic Research Foundation and Students For Liberty. Like Atlas, we at SFL believe that ideas know no borders. Our affiliates around the world work to promote free and just societies. We are young idealists who know that liberty is not only beautiful and inspiring, but that it works in practice. We, the youth, are taking up the task of educating ourselves and our fellow students about the great issues of freedom, justice, prosperity, and peace. We build on foundations built by generations of thinkers, entrepreneurs, activists, and scholars.

This movement is diverse. Our members speak many languages, profess many religions, and come from many nations, but we are united by our common principles: economic freedom to choose how to provide for oneself, social freedom to choose how to live one's life, and intellectual and academic freedom. We believe that freedom does not come in pieces, but rather that it is a single and indivisible concept that must be defended at all times.

Why *The Economics of Freedom*? Because at present, fallacious economic thought is being used to justify the steady erosion of our freedoms. The examples are plentiful: "stimulus packages" that pile debt on top of debt; increased military spending in the name of "job creation"; foolish destruction of wealth ("cash for clunkers") to benefit powerful industries; trade obstructions (quotas and tariffs) that benefit the few at the expense of the many and undermine international peace; phony "regulations" that do not make things "regular," but instead disrupt and disorder economies; and confiscation, nationalization, and plunder. All are in vogue among the political classes.

Our generation is not the first to be confronted by such fallacies. Frédéric Bastiat destroyed the very same economic fallacies many generations ago. Bastiat was a nineteenth century French political economist who dedicated the last years of his short life to proving that government by its nature possesses neither the moral authority to intervene in our freedom nor the practical ability to create prosperity through its intervention.

The Economics of Freedom presents some of Bastiat's most important essays. They reveal a sharp mind systematically debunking one fallacy after another and a moral conscience that recoiled from violence and tyranny. To read and understand "What Is Seen and What Is Not Seen" is to contemplate the world in a new light. It is one of the most important essays ever written in economics. In addition to Bastiat's writings, this book includes two essays that show the importance of Bastiat's ideas and then update and apply them to more contemporary issues.

The Foreword to Bastiat's essays was written by the 1974 Nobel Laureate in economic science, F.A. Hayek. Hayek was not only a pioneer of economic thought who gained fame for his work showing why socialism fails and how markets utilize dispersed knowledge (see his essay on "The Use of Knowledge in Society," which is available online at www.econlib.org, and his Nobel lecture, which is available at NobelPrize.org). He was also a forceful champion of liberty. *The Road to Serfdom*, published in 1944 in England, has become a classic of political thought, as have *The Constitution of Liberty* and *Law, Legislation, and Liberty*.

The concluding essay, "Twenty Myths about Markets" by Dr. Tom G. Palmer, was first delivered in 2007 in Nairobi, Kenya, at a meeting of the Mont Pelerin Society, the international society that Hayek founded in 1947. Dr. Palmer is a senior fellow at the Cato Institute and vice president of the Atlas Economic Research Foundation, a worldwide network of think tanks. Palmer formulates, considers, and refutes the myths that pass for wisdom, including even some "overly enthusiastic defenses" of markets that misstate their nature.

The academy is, perhaps unsurprisingly, full of people who think that they are smart enough to run the lives of others. They are not. Hence the subtitle of this volume: "What Your Professors Won't Tell You." While your teachers likely value freedom, they too often overlook the broader implications of government intervention, particularly in the economic sphere. Because they overestimate their own intellectual powers, they ignore the "unintended consequences" of intervention into the voluntary interactions of others. Nor do they understand that the theories they propound are too often deployed by special interests, which are better at manipulating and abusing power than are university professors. That is why we at Students For Liberty have taken up this cause, because if we do not advocate liberty in all of its forms, who will?

We believe that a free society demands respect for the freedom of everyone to pursue his or her own goals and to trade ideas, goods, and services on voluntarily agreed-to terms. When all enjoy equal freedom and our interactions are voluntary, the result is not chaos, but order; not poverty, but plenty; not conflict, but cooperation.

We hope this book has made it into the hands of a curious student with an open mind. If you find the ideas of this book interesting, you can visit www.studentsforliberty.org to learn more about the student movement for liberty and join the fight for a free academy and a free society.

Foreword

by F. A. Hayek

Even those who may question the eminence of Frédéric Bastiat as an economic theorist will grant that he was a publicist of genius. Joseph Schumpeter calls him "the most brilliant economic journalist who ever lived." For the purpose of introducing the present volume, which contains some of the most successful of his writings for the general public, we might well leave it at that. One might even grant Schumpeter's harsh assessment of Bastiat that "he was not a theorist" without seriously diminishing his stature. It is true that when, at the end of his extremely short career as a writer, he attempted to provide a theoretical justification for his general conceptions, he did not satisfy the professionals. It would indeed have been a miracle if a man who, after only five years as a regular writer on public affairs, attempted in a few months, and with a mortal illness rapidly closing in on him, to defend the points on which he differed from established doctrine, had fully succeeded in this too. Yet one may ask whether it was not only his early death at the age of forty-nine that prevented him. His polemical writings, which in consequence are the most important ones he has left, certainly prove that he had an insight into what was significant and a gift for going to the heart of the matter that would have provided him with ample material for real contributions to science.

Nothing illustrates this better than the celebrated title of the first essay in the present volume. "What is seen and what is not seen in political economy!" No one has ever stated more clearly in a single phrase the central difficulty of a rational economic policy and, I would like to add, the decisive argument for economic freedom. It is the idea compressed into these few words that made me use the word "genius" in the opening sentence. It is indeed a text around which one might expound a whole system of libertarian economic policy. And though it constitutes the title for only the first essay in this volume, it provides the leading idea for all. Bastiat illustrates its meaning over and over again in refuting the current fallacies of his time. I shall later indicate that, though the views he combats are today usually advanced only in a more sophisticated guise, they have basically not changed very much since Bastiat's time. But first I want to say a few words about the more general significance of his central idea.

This is simply that if we judge measures of economic policy solely by their immediate and concretely foreseeable effects, we shall not only not achieve a viable order but shall be certain progressively to extinguish freedom and thereby prevent more good than our measures will produce. Freedom is important in order that all the different individuals can make full use of the particular circumstances of which only they know. We therefore never know what beneficial actions we prevent if we restrict their freedom to serve their fellows in whatever manner they wish. All acts of interference, however, amount to such restrictions. They are, of course, always undertaken to achieve some definite objective. Against the foreseen direct results of such actions of government we shall in each individual case be able to balance only the mere probability that some unknown but beneficial actions by some individuals will be prevented. In consequence, if such decisions are made from case to case and not governed by an attachment to freedom as a general principle, freedom is bound to lose in almost every case. Bastiat was indeed right in treating freedom of choice as a moral principle that must never be sacrificed to considerations of expediency; because there is perhaps no aspect of freedom that would not be abolished if it were to be respected only where the concrete damage caused by its abolition can be pointed out.

Bastiat directed his arguments against certain ever-recurring fallacies as they were employed in his time. Few people would employ them today quite as naively as it was still possible to do then. But let the reader not deceive himself that these same fallacies no longer play an important role in contemporary economic discussion: they are today expressed merely in a more sophisticated form and are therefore more difficult to detect. The reader who has learnt to recognize these stock fallacies in their simpler manifestations will at least be on his guard when he finds the same conclusions derived from what appears to be a more scientific argument. It is characteristic of much of recent economics that by ever new arguments it has tried to vindicate those very prejudices which are so attractive because the maxims that follow from them are so pleasant or convenient: spending is a good thing, and saving is bad; waste benefits and economy harms the mass of the people; money will do more good in the hands of the government than in those of the people; it is the duty of government to see that everybody gets what he deserves; etc., etc.

None of these ideas has lost any of its power in our time. The only difference is that Bastiat, in combating them, was on the whole fighting on the side of the professional economists against popular beliefs exploited by interested parties, while similar proposals are today propagated by an influential school of economists in a most impressive and, to the layman, largely unintelligible garb. It is doubtful whether there is one among the fallacies which one might have hoped Bastiat had killed once and for all that has not experienced its resurrection. I shall give only one example. To an account of Bastiat's best-known economic fable, The Petition of the Candlemakers against the Competition of the Sun, in which it is demanded that windows should be prohibited because of the benefit which the prosperity of the candlemakers would confer on everyone else, a well-known French textbook of the history of economics adds in its latest edition the following footnote: "It should be noted that according to Keynes—on the assumption of underemployment and in accordance with the theory of the multiplier—this argument of the candlemakers is literally and fully valid."

The attentive reader will notice that, while Bastiat grapples with so many economic panaceas which are familiar to us, one of the main dangers of our time does not appear in his pages. Though he has to deal with various queer proposals for using credit which were current in his time, straight inflation through a government deficit seemed in his age not a major danger. An increase of expenditure means for him necessarily and immediately an increase in taxation. The reason is that, as among all people who have gone through a major inflation within living memory, a continuous depreciation of money was not a thing with which people would have put up with in his day. So if the reader should be inclined to feel superior to the rather simple fallacies that Bastiat often finds it necessary to refute, he should remember that in some other respects his compatriots of more than a hundred years ago were considerably wiser than our generation.

F.A. Hayek

What Is Seen and What Is Not Seen

by Frédéric Bastiat

In the economic sphere an act, a habit, an institution, a law produces not only one effect, but a series of effects. Of these effects, the first alone is immediate; it appears simultaneously with its cause; *it is seen*. The other effects emerge only subsequently; *they are not seen*; we are fortunate if we *foresee* them.

There is only one difference between a bad economist and a good one: the bad economist confines himself to the *visible* effect; the good economist takes into account both the effect that can be seen and those effects that must be *foreseen*.

Yet this difference is tremendous, for it almost always happens that when the immediate consequence is favorable, the later consequences are disastrous, and vice versa. Whence it follows that the bad economist pursues a small present good that will be followed by a great evil to come, while the good economist pursues a great good to come, at the risk of a small present evil.

The same thing, of course, is true of health and morals. Often, the sweeter the first fruit of a habit, the more bitter are its later fruits: for example, debauchery, sloth, prodigality. When a man is impressed by the effect *that is seen* and has not yet learned to discern the effects *that are not seen,* he indulges in deplorable habits, not only through natural inclination, but deliberately.

This explains man's necessarily painful evolution. Ignorance surrounds him at his cradle; therefore, he regulates his acts according to their first consequences, the only ones that, in his infancy, he can see. It is only after a long time that he learns to take account of the others. Two very different masters teach him this lesson: experience and foresight. Experience teaches efficaciously but brutally. It instructs us in all the effects of an act by making us feel them, and we cannot fail to learn eventually, from having been burned ourselves, that fire burns. I should prefer, insofar as possible, to replace this rude teacher with one more gentle: foresight. For that reason I shall investigate the consequences of several economic phenomena, contrasting those *that are seen* with those *that are not seen*.

1. The Broken Window

Have you ever been witness to the fury of that solid citizen, James Goodfellow, when his incorrigible son has happened to break a pane of glass? If you have been present at this spectacle, certainly you must also have observed that the onlookers, even if there are as many as thirty of them, seem with one accord to offer the unfortunate owner the selfsame consolation: "It's an ill wind that blows nobody some good. Such accidents keep industry going. Everybody has to make a living. What would become of the glaziers if no one ever broke a window?"

Now, this formula of condolence contains a whole theory that it is a good idea for us to expose, *flagrante delicto,* in this very simple case, since it is exactly the same as that which, unfortunately, underlies most of our economic institutions.

Suppose that it will cost six francs to repair the damage. If you mean that the accident gives six francs' worth of encouragement to the aforesaid industry, I agree. I do not contest it in any way; your reasoning is correct. The glazier will come, do his job, receive six francs, congratulate himself, and bless in his heart the careless child. *That is what is seen.*

But if, by way of deduction, you conclude, as happens only too often, that it is good to break windows, that it helps to circulate money, that it results in encouraging industry in general, I am obliged to cry out: That will never do! Your theory stops at *what is seen.* It does not take account of *what is not seen.*

It is not seen that, since our citizen has spent six francs for one thing, he will not be able to spend them for another. *It is not seen* that if he had not had a windowpane to replace, he would have replaced, for example, his worn-out shoes or added another book to his library. In brief, he would have put his six francs to some use or other for which he will not now have them.

Let us next consider industry *in general.* The window having been broken, the glass industry gets six francs' worth of encouragement; *that is what is seen.*

If the window had not been broken, the shoe industry (or some other) would have received six francs' worth of encouragement; *that is what is not seen.*

And if we were to take into consideration *what is not seen,* because it is a negative factor, as well as *what is seen,* because it is a positive factor, we should understand that there is no benefit to industry *in general* or to *national employment* as a whole, whether windows are broken or not broken.

Now let us consider James Goodfellow.

On the first hypothesis, that of the broken window, he spends six francs and has, neither more nor less than before, the enjoyment of one window.

On the second, that in which the accident did not happen, he would have spent six francs for new shoes and would have had the enjoyment of a pair of shoes as well as of a window.

Now, if James Goodfellow is part of society, we must conclude that society, considering its labors and its enjoyments, has lost the value of the broken window.

From which, by generalizing, we arrive at this unexpected conclusion: "Society loses the value of objects unnecessarily destroyed," and at this aphorism, which will make the hair of the protectionists stand on end: "To break, to destroy, to dissipate is not to encourage national employment," or more briefly: "Destruction is not profitable."

What will the *Moniteur industriel* say to this, or the disciples of the estimable M. de Saint-Chamans, who has calculated with such precision what industry would gain from the burning of Paris, because of the houses that would have to be rebuilt?

I am sorry to upset his ingenious calculations, especially since their spirit has passed into our legislation. But I beg him to begin them again, entering *what is not seen* in the ledger beside *what is seen.*

The reader must apply himself to observe that there are not only two people, but three, in the little drama that I have presented. The one, James Goodfellow, represents the consumer, reduced by destruction to one enjoyment instead of two. The other, under the figure of the glazier, shows us the producer whose industry the accident encourages. The third is the shoemaker (or any other manufacturer) whose industry is correspondingly discouraged by the same cause. It is this third person who is always in the shadow, and who, personifying *what is not seen,* is an essential element of the problem. It is he who makes us understand how absurd it is to see a profit in destruction. It is he who will soon teach us that it is equally absurd to see a profit in trade restriction, which is, after all, nothing more nor less than partial destruction. So, if you get to the bottom of all the arguments advanced in favor of restrictionist measures, you will find only a paraphrase of that common cliché: *"What would become of the glaziers if no one ever broke any windows?"*

2. The Demobilization

A nation is in the same case as a man. When a man wishes to give himself a satisfaction, he has to see whether it is worth what it costs. For a nation, security is the greatest of blessings. If, to acquire it, a hundred thousand men must be mobilized, and a hundred million francs spent, I have nothing to say. It is an enjoyment bought at the price of a sacrifice.

Let there be no misunderstanding, then, about the point I wish to make in what I have to say on this subject.

A legislator proposes to discharge a hundred thousand men, which will relieve the taxpayers of a hundred million francs in taxes.

Suppose we confine ourselves to replying to him: "These one hundred thousand men and these one hundred million francs are indispensable to our national security. It is a sacrifice; but without this sacrifice France would be torn by internal factions or invaded from without." I have no objection here to this argument, which may be true or false as the case may be, but which theoretically does not constitute any economic heresy. The heresy begins when the sacrifice itself is represented as an advantage, because it brings profit to someone.

Now, if I am not mistaken, no sooner will the author of the proposal have descended from the platform, than an orator will rush up and say:

"Discharge a hundred thousand men! What are you thinking of? What will become of them? What will they live on? On their earnings? But do you not know that there is unemployment everywhere? That all occupations are oversupplied? Do you wish to throw them on the market to increase the competition and to depress wage rates? Just at the moment when it is difficult to earn a meager living, is it not fortunate that the state is giving bread to a hundred thousand individuals? Consider further that the army consumes wine, clothes, and weapons, that it thus spreads business to the factories and the garrison towns, and that it is nothing less than a godsend to its innumerable suppliers. Do you not tremble at the idea of bringing this immense industrial activity to an end?"

This speech, we see, concludes in favor of maintaining a hundred thousand soldiers, not because of the nation's need for the services rendered by the army, but for economic reasons. It is these considerations alone that I propose to refute.

A hundred thousand men, costing the taxpayers a hundred million francs, live as well and provide as good a living for their suppliers as a hundred million francs will allow; *that is what is seen.*

But a hundred million francs, coming from the pockets of the taxpayers, ceases to provide a living for these taxpayers and *their* suppliers, to the extent of a hundred million francs; *that is what is not seen.* Calculate, figure, and tell me where there is any profit for the mass of the people.

I will, for my part, tell you where the *loss* is, and to simplify things, instead of speaking of a hundred thousand men and a hundred million francs, let us talk about one man and a thousand francs.

Here we are in the village of A. The recruiters make the rounds and muster one man. The tax collectors make their rounds also and raise a thousand francs. The man and the sum are transported to Metz, the one destined to keep the other alive for a year without doing anything. If you look only at Metz, yes, you are right a hundred times; the procedure is very advantageous. But if you turn your eyes to the village of A, you will judge otherwise, for, unless you are blind, you will see that this village has lost a laborer and the thousand francs that would remunerate his labor, and the business which, through the spending of these thousand francs, he would spread about him.

At first glance it seems as if the loss is compensated. What took place at the village now takes place at Metz, and that is all there is to it. But here is where the loss is. In the village a man dug and labored: he was a worker; at Metz he goes through "Right dress!" and "Left dress!": he is a soldier. The money involved and its circulation are the same in both cases: but in one there were three hundred days of productive labor; in the other there are three hundreds days of unproductive labor, on the supposition, of course, that a part of the army is not indispensable to public security.

Now comes demobilization. You point out to me a surplus of a hundred thousand workers, intensified competition and the pressure that it exerts on wage rates. That is what you see.

But here is what you do not see. You do not see that to send home a hundred thousand soldiers is not to do away with a hundred million francs, but to return that money to the taxpayers. You do not see that to throw a hundred thousand workers on the market in this way is to throw in at the same time the hundred million francs destined to pay for their labor; that, as a consequence, the same measure that increases the *supply* of workers also increases the *demand;* from which it follows that your lowering of wages is illusory. You do not see that before, as well as after, the demobilization there are a hundred million francs corresponding to the hundred thousand men; that the whole difference consists in this: that before, the country gives the hundred million francs to the hundred thousand men for doing nothing; afterwards, it gives them the money for working. Finally, you do not see that when a taxpayer gives his money, whether to a soldier in exchange for nothing or to a worker in exchange for something, all the more remote consequences of the circulation of this money are the same in both cases: only, in the second case the taxpayer receives something; in the first he receives nothing. Result: a dead loss for the nation.

The sophism that I am attacking here cannot withstand the test of extended application, which is the touchstone of all theoretical principles. If, all things considered, there is a *national profit* in increasing the size of the army, why not call the whole male population of the country to the colors?

3. Taxes

Have you ever heard anyone say: "Taxes are the best investment; they are a life-giving dew. See how many families they keep alive, and follow in imagination their indirect effects on industry; they are infinite, as extensive as life itself."

To combat this doctrine, I am obliged to repeat the preceding refutation. Political economy knows very well that its arguments are not diverting enough for anyone to say about them: *Repetita placent*; repetition pleases. So, like Basile, political economy has "arranged" the proverb for its own use, quite convinced that, from its mouth, *Repetita docent*; repetition teaches.

The advantages that government officials enjoy in drawing their salaries are *what is seen*. The benefits that result for their suppliers are also *what is seen*. They are right under your nose.

But the disadvantage that the taxpayers try to free themselves from is *what is not seen*, and the distress that results from it for the merchants who supply them is *something further that is not seen*, although it should stand out plainly enough to be seen intellectually.

When a government official spends on his own behalf one hundred sous more, this implies that a taxpayer spends on his own behalf one hundred sous the less. But the spending of the government official is *seen*, because it is done; while that of the taxpayer *is not seen*, because—alas!—he is prevented from doing it.

You compare the nation to a parched piece of land and the tax to a life-giving rain. So be it. But you should also ask yourself where this rain comes from, and whether it is not precisely the tax that draws the moisture from the soil and dries it up.

You should ask yourself further whether the soil receives more of this precious water from the rain than it loses by the evaporation?

What is quite certain is that, when James Goodfellow counts out a hundred sous to the tax collector, he receives nothing in return. When, then, a government official, in spending these hundred sous, returns them to James Goodfellow, it is for an equivalent value in wheat or in labor. The final result is a loss of five francs for James Goodfellow.

It is quite true that often, nearly always if you will, the government official renders an equivalent service to James Goodfellow. In this case there is no loss on either side; there is only an exchange. Therefore, my argument is not in any way concerned with useful functions. I say this: If you wish to create a government office, prove its usefulness. Demonstrate that to James Goodfellow it is worth the equivalent of what it costs him by virtue of the services it renders him. But apart from this intrinsic utility, do not cite, as an argument in favor of opening the new bureau, the advantage that it constitutes for the bureaucrat, his family, and those who supply his needs; do not allege that it encourages employment.

When James Goodfellow gives a hundred sous to a government official for a really useful service, this is exactly the same as when he gives a hundred sous to a shoemaker for a pair of shoes. It is a case of give-and-take, and the score is even. But when James Goodfellow hands over a hundred sous to a government official to receive no service for it or even to be subjected to inconveniences, it is as if he were to give his money to a thief. It serves no purpose to say that the official will spend these hundred sous for the great profit of our *national industry*; the more the thief can do with them, the more James Goodfellow could have done with them if he had not met on his way either the extralegal or the legal parasite.

Let us accustom ourselves, then, not to judge things solely by *what is seen,* but rather by *what is not seen*.

Last year I was on the Finance Committee, for in the Constituent Assembly the members of the opposition were not systematically excluded from all committees. In this the framers of the Constitution acted wisely. We have heard M. Thiers say: "I have spent my life fighting men of the legitimist party and of the clerical party. Since, in the face of a common danger, I have come to know them and we have had heart-to-heart talks, I see that they are not the monsters I had imagined."

Yes, enmities become exaggerated and hatreds are intensified between parties that do not mingle; and if the majority would allow a few members of the minority to penetrate into the circles of the committees, perhaps it would be recognized on both sides that their ideas are not so far apart, and above all that their intentions are not so perverse, as supposed.

However that may be, last year I was on the Finance Committee. Each time that one of our colleagues spoke of fixing at a moderate figure the salaries of the President of the Republic, of cabinet ministers, and of ambassadors, he would be told:

"For the good of the service, we must surround certain offices with an aura of prestige and dignity. That is the way to attract to them men of merit. Innumerable unfortunate people turn to the President of the Republic, and he would be in a painful position if he were always forced to refuse them help. A certain amount of ostentation in the ministerial and diplomatic salons is part of the machinery of constitutional governments, etc., etc."

Whether or not such arguments can be controverted, they certainly deserve serious scrutiny. They are based on the public interest, rightly or wrongly estimated; and, personally, I can make more of a case for them than many of our Catos, moved by a narrow spirit of niggardliness or jealousy.

But what shocks my economist's conscience, what makes me blush for the intellectual renown of my country, is when they go on from these arguments (as they never fail to do) to this absurd banality (always favorably received):

"Besides, the luxury of high officials of the government encourages the arts, industry, and employment. The Chief of State and his ministers cannot give banquets and parties without infusing life into all the veins of the body politic. To reduce their salaries would be to starve industry in Paris and, at the same time, throughout the nation."

For heaven's sake, gentlemen, at least respect arithmetic, and do not come before the National Assembly of France and say, for fear that, to its shame, it will not support you, that an addition gives a different sum depending upon whether it is added from top to bottom or from bottom to top.

Well, then, suppose I arrange to have a navvy dig me a ditch in my field for the sum of a hundred sous. Just as I conclude this agreement, the tax collector takes my hundred sous from me and has them passed on to the Minister of the Interior. My contract is broken, but the Minister will add another dish at his dinner. On what basis do you dare to affirm that this official expenditure is an addition to the national industry? Do you not see that it is only a simple *transfer* of consumption and of labor? A cabinet minister has his table more lavishly set, it is true; but a farmer has his field less well drained, and this is just as true. A Parisian caterer has gained a hundred sous, I grant you; but grant me that a provincial ditchdigger has lost five francs. All that one can say is that the official dish and the satisfied caterer are *what is seen;* the swampy field and the excavator out of work are *what is not seen.*

Good Lord! What a lot of trouble to prove in political economy that two and two make four; and if you succeed in doing so, people cry, "It is so clear that it is boring." Then they vote as if you had never proved anything at all.

4. Theaters and Fine Arts

Should the state subsidize the arts?

There is certainly a great deal to say on this subject pro and con.

In favor of the system of subsidies, one can say that the arts broaden, elevate, and poetize the soul of a nation; that they draw it away from material preoccupations, giving it a feeling for the beautiful, and thus react favorably on its manners, its customs, its morals, and even on its industry. One can ask where music would be in France without the Théâtre-Italien and the Conservatory; dramatic art without the Théâtre-Français; painting and sculpture without our collections and our museums. One can go further and ask whether, without the centralization and consequently the subsidizing of the fine arts, there would have developed that exquisite taste which is the noble endowment of French labor and sends its products out over the whole world. In the presence of such results would it not be the height of imprudence to renounce this moderate assessment on all the citizens, which, in the last analysis, is what has achieved for them their pre-eminence and their glory in the eyes of Europe?

To these reasons and many others, whose power I do not contest, one can oppose many no less cogent. There is, first of all, one could say, a question of distributive justice. Do the rights of the legislator go so far as to allow him to dip into the wages of the artisan in order to supplement the profits of the artist? M. de

Lamartine said: "If you take away the subsidy of a theater, where are you going to stop on this path, and will you not be logically required to do away with your university faculties, your museums, your institutes, your libraries?" One could reply: If you wish to subsidize all that is good and useful, where are you going to stop on *that* path, and will you not logically be required to set up a civil list for agriculture, industry, commerce, welfare, and education? Furthermore, is it certain that subsidies favor the progress of the arts? It is a question that is far from being resolved, and we see with our own eyes that the theaters that prosper are those that live on their own profits. Finally, proceeding to higher considerations, one may observe that needs and desires give rise to one another and keep soaring into regions more and more rarefied in proportion as the national wealth permits their satisfaction; that the government must not meddle in this process, since, whatever may be currently the amount of the national wealth, it cannot stimulate luxury industries by taxation without harming essential industries, thus reversing the natural advance of civilization. One may also point out that this artificial dislocation of wants, tastes, labor, and population places nations in a precarious and dangerous situation, leaving them without a solid base.

These are some of the reasons alleged by the adversaries of state intervention concerning the order in which citizens believe they should satisfy their needs and their desires, and thus direct their activity. I confess that I am one of those who think that the choice, the impulse, should come from below, not from above, from the citizens, not from the legislator; and the contrary doctrine seems to me to lead to the annihilation of liberty and of human dignity.

But, by an inference as false as it is unjust, do you know what the economists are now accused of? When we oppose subsidies, we are charged with opposing the very thing that it was proposed to subsidize and of being the enemies of all kinds of activity, because we want these activities to be voluntary and to seek their proper reward in themselves. Thus, if we ask that the state not intervene, by taxation, in religious matters, we are atheists. If we ask that the state not intervene, by taxation, in education, then we hate enlightenment. If we say that the state should not give, by taxation, an artificial value to land or to some branch of industry, then we are the enemies of property and of labor. If we think that the state should not subsidize artists, we are barbarians who judge the arts useless.

I protest with all my power against these inferences. Far from entertaining the absurd thought of abolishing religion, education, property, labor, and the arts when we ask the state to protect the free development of all these types of human activity without keeping them on the payroll at one another's expense, we believe, on the contrary, that all these vital forces of society should develop harmoniously under the influence of liberty and that none of them should become, as we see has happened today, a source of trouble, abuses, tyranny, and disorder.

Our adversaries believe that an activity that is neither subsidized nor regulated is abolished. We believe the contrary. Their faith is in the legislator, not in mankind. Ours is in mankind, not in the legislator.

Thus, M. de Lamartine said: "On the basis of this principle, we should have to *abolish* the public expositions that bring wealth and honor to this country."

I reply to M. de Lamartine: From your point of view, *not to subsidize* is *to abolish,* because, proceeding from the premise that nothing exists except by the will of the state, you conclude that nothing lives that taxes do not keep alive. But I turn against you the example that you have chosen, and I point out to you that the greatest, the noblest, of all expositions, the one based on the most liberal, the most universal conception, and I can even use the word "humanitarian," which is not here exaggerated, is the exposition now being prepared in London, the only one in which no government meddles and which no tax supports.

Returning to the fine arts, one can, I repeat, allege weighty reasons for and against the system of subsidization. The reader understands that, in accordance with the special purpose of this essay, I have no need either to set forth these reasons or to decide between them.

But M. de Lamartine has advanced one argument that I cannot pass over in silence, for it falls within the very carefully defined limits of this economic study. He has said:

The economic question in the matter of theaters can be summed up in one word: employment. The nature of the employment matters little; it is of a kind just as productive and fertile as any other kind. The theaters, as you know, support by wages no less than eighty thousand workers of all kinds—painters, masons, decorators, costumers, architects, etc., who are the very life and industry of many quarters of this capital, and they should have this claim upon your sympathies!

Your sympathies? Translate: your subsidies.

And further on:

The pleasures of Paris provide employment and consumers' goods for the provincial departments, and the luxuries of the rich are the wages and the bread of two hundred thousand workers of all kinds, living on the complex industry of the theaters throughout the Republic, and receiving from these noble pleasures, which make France illustrious, their own livelihood and the means of providing the necessities of life for their families and their children. It is to them that you give these sixty thousand francs. [*Very good! Very good! Much applause.*]

For my part, I am forced to say: *Very bad! Very bad!* confining, of course, the burden of this judgment to the economic argument which we are here concerned with.

Yes, it is, at least in part, to the workers in the theaters that the sixty thousand francs in question will go. A few scraps might well get lost on the way. If one scrutinized the matter closely, one might even discover that most of the pie will find its way elsewhere. The workers will be fortunate if there are a few crumbs left for them! But I should like to assume that the entire subsidy will go to the painters, decorators, costumers, hairdressers, etc. *That is what is seen.*

But where does it come from? This is the *other side* of the coin, just as important to examine as its *face*. What is the source of these 60,000 francs? And where *would they have gone* if a legislative vote had not first directed them to the rue de Rivoli and from there to the rue de Grenelle? *That is what is not seen.*

Surely, no one will dare maintain that the legislative vote has caused this sum to hatch out from the ballot box; that it is a pure addition to the national wealth; that, without this miraculous vote, these sixty thousand francs would have remained invisible and impalpable. It must be admitted that all that the majority can do is to decide that they will be taken from somewhere to be sent somewhere else, and that they will have one destination only by being deflected from another.

This being the case, it is clear that the taxpayer who will have been taxed one franc will no longer have this franc at his disposal. It is clear that he will be deprived of a satisfaction to the tune of one franc, and that the worker, whoever he is, who would have procured this satisfaction for him, will be deprived of wages in the same amount.

Let us not, then, yield to the childish illusion of believing that the vote of May 16 *adds* anything whatever to national well-being and employment. It reallocates possessions, it reallocates wages, and that is all.

Will it be said that for one kind of satisfaction and for one kind of job it substitutes satisfactions and jobs more urgent, more moral, more rational? I could do battle on this ground. I could say: In taking sixty thousand francs from the taxpayers, you reduce the wages of plowmen, ditchdiggers, carpenters, and blacksmiths, and you increase by the same amount the wages of singers, hairdressers, decorators, and costumers. Nothing proves that this latter class is more important than the other. M. de Lamartine does not make this allegation. He says himself that the work of the theaters is *just as* productive as, *just as* fruitful as, and not *more so* than, any other work, which might still be contested; for the best proof that theatrical work is not as productive as other work is that the latter is called upon to subsidize the former.

But this comparison of the intrinsic value and merit of the different kinds of work forms no part of my present subject. All that I have to do here is to show that, if M. de Lamartine and those who have applauded his argument have seen on the one hand the wages earned by those who supply the needs of the actors, they should see on the other the earnings lost by those who supply the needs of the taxpayers; if they do not, they are open to ridicule for mistaking a reallocation for a *gain*. If they were logical in their doctrine, they would ask for infinite subsidies; for what is true of one franc and of sixty thousand francs is true, in identical circumstances, of a billion francs.

When it is a question of taxes, gentlemen, prove their usefulness by reasons with some foundation, but not with that lamentable assertion: "Public spending keeps the working class alive." It makes the mistake of covering up a fact that it is essential to know: namely, that *public spending* is *always* a substitute for *private spending*, and that consequently it may well support one worker in place of another but adds nothing to the lot of the working class taken as a whole. Your argument is fashionable, but it is quite absurd, for the reasoning is not correct.

5. Public Works

Nothing is more natural than that a nation, after making sure that a great enterprise will profit the community, should have such an enterprise carried out with funds collected from the citizenry. But I lose patience completely, I confess, when I hear alleged in support of such a resolution this economic fallacy: "Besides, it is a way of creating jobs for the workers."

The state opens a road, builds a palace, repairs a street, digs a canal; with these projects it gives jobs to certain workers. *That is what is seen.* But it deprives certain other laborers of employment. *That is what is not seen.*

Suppose a road is under construction. A thousand laborers arrive every morning, go home every evening, and receive their wages; that is certain. If the road had not been authorized, if funds for it had not been voted, these good people would have neither found this work nor earned these wages; that again is certain.

But is this all? Taken all together, does not the operation involve something else? At the moment when M. Dupin pronounces the sacramental words: "The Assembly has adopted . . ." do millions of francs descend miraculously on a moonbeam into the coffers of M. Fould and M. Bineau? For the process to be complete, does not the state have to organize the collection of funds as well as their expenditure? Does it not have to get its tax collectors into the country and its taxpayers to make their contribution?

Study the question, then, from its two aspects. In noting what the state is going to do with the millions of francs voted, do not neglect to note also what the taxpayers would have done—and can no longer do—with these same millions. You see, then, that a public enterprise is a coin with two sides. On one, the figure of a busy worker, with this device: *What is seen*; on the other, an unemployed worker, with this device: *What is not seen*.

The sophism that I am attacking in this essay is all the more dangerous when applied to public works, since it serves to justify the most foolishly prodigal enterprises. When a railroad or a bridge has real utility, it suffices to rely on this fact in arguing in its favor. But if one cannot do this, what does one do? One has recourse to this mumbo jumbo: "We must create jobs for the workers."

This means that the terraces of the Champ-de-Mars are ordered first to be built up and then to be torn down. The great Napoleon, it is said, thought he was doing philanthropic work when he had ditches dug and then filled in. He also said: "What difference does the result make? All we need is to see wealth spread among the laboring classes."

Let us get to the bottom of things. Money creates an illusion for us. To ask for cooperation, in the form of money, from all the citizens in a common enterprise is, in reality, to ask of them actual physical co-operation, for each one of them procures for himself by his labor the amount he is taxed. Now, if we were to gather together all the citizens and exact their services from them in order to have a piece of work performed that is useful to all, this would be understandable; their recompense would consist in the results of the work itself. But if, after being brought together, they were forced to build roads on which no one would travel, or palaces that no one would live in, all under the pretext of providing work for them, it would seem absurd, and they would certainly be justified in objecting: We will have none of that kind of work. We would rather work for ourselves.

Having the citizens contribute money, and not labor, changes nothing in the general results. But if labor were contributed, the loss would be shared by everyone. Where money is contributed, those whom the state keeps busy escape their share of the loss, while adding much more to that which their compatriots already have to suffer.

There is an article in the Constitution which states:

"Society assists and encourages the development of labor . . . through the establishment by the state, the departments, and the municipalities, of appropriate public works to employ idle hands."

As a temporary measure in a time of crisis, during a severe winter, this intervention on the part of the taxpayer could have good effects. It acts in the same way as insurance. It adds nothing to the number of jobs nor to total wages, but it takes labor and wages from ordinary times and doles them out, at a loss it is true, in difficult times.

As a permanent, general, systematic measure, it is nothing but a ruinous hoax, an impossibility, a contradiction, which makes a great show of the little work that it has stimulated, which is *what is seen,* and conceals the much larger amount of work that it has precluded, which is *what is not seen.*

6. Middlemen

Society is the aggregate of all the services that men perform for one another by compulsion or voluntarily, that is to say, *public services* and *private services.*

The first, imposed and regulated by the law, which is not always easy to change when necessary, can long outlive their usefulness and still retain the name of *public services,* even when they are no longer anything but public nuisances. The second are in the domain of the voluntary, i.e., of individual responsibility. Each gives and receives what he wishes, or what he can, after bargaining. These services are always presumed to have a real utility, exactly measured by their comparative value.

That is why the former are so often static, while the latter obey the law of progress.

While the exaggerated development of public services, with the waste of energies that it entails, tends to create a disastrous parasitism in society, it is rather strange that many modern schools of economic thought, attributing this characteristic to voluntary, private services, seek to transform the functions performed by the various occupations.

These schools of thought are vehement in their attack on those they call middlemen. They would willingly eliminate the capitalist, the banker, the speculator, the entrepreneur, the businessman, and the merchant, accusing them of interposing themselves between producer and consumer in order to fleece them both, without giving them anything of value. Or rather, the reformers would like to transfer to the state the work of the middlemen, for this work cannot be eliminated.

The sophism of the socialists on this point consists in showing the public what it pays to the *middlemen* for their services and in concealing what would have to be paid to the state. Once again we have the conflict between what strikes the eye and what is evidenced only to the mind, between *what is seen and what is not seen*.

It was especially in 1847 and on the occasion of the famine that the socialist schools succeeded in popularizing their disastrous theory. They knew well that the most absurd propaganda always has some chance with men who are suffering; *malesuada fames*.

Then, with the aid of those high-sounding words: *Exploitation of man by man, speculation in hunger, monopoly,* they set themselves to blackening the name of business and throwing a veil over its benefits.

"Why," they said, "leave to merchants the task of getting food-stuffs from the United States and the Crimea? Why cannot the state, the departments, and the municipalities organize a provisioning service and set up warehouses for stockpiling? They would sell at *net cost*, and the people, the poor people, would be relieved of the tribute that they pay to free—i.e., selfish, individualistic, anarchical—trade."

The tribute that the people pay to business, *is what is seen.* The tribute that the people would have to pay to the state or to its agents in the socialist system, *is what is not seen.*

What is this so-called tribute that people pay to business? It is this: that two men render each other a service in full freedom under the pressure of competition and at a price agreed on after bargaining.

When the stomach that is hungry is in Paris and the wheat that can satisfy it is in Odessa, the suffering will not cease until the wheat reaches the stomach. There are three ways to accomplish this: the hungry men can go themselves to find the wheat; they can put their trust in those who engage in this kind of business; or they can levy an assessment on themselves and charge public officials with the task.

Of these three methods, which is the most advantageous?

In all times, in all countries, the freer, the more enlightened, the more experienced men have been, the oftener have they *voluntarily* chosen the second. I confess that this is enough in my eyes to give the advantage to it. My mind refuses to admit that mankind at large deceives itself on a point that touches it so closely.

However, let us examine the question.

For thirty-six million citizens to depart for Odessa to get the wheat that they need is obviously impracticable. The first means is of no avail. The consumers cannot act by themselves; they are compelled to turn to middlemen, whether public officials or merchants.

However, let us observe that the first means would be the most natural. Fundamentally, it is the responsibility of whoever is hungry to get his own wheat. It is a *task* that concerns him; it is a *service* that he owes to himself. If someone else, whoever he may be, performs this *service* for him and takes the task on himself, this other person has a right to compensation. What I am saying here is that the services of *middlemen* involve a right to remuneration.

However that may be, since we must turn to what the socialists call a parasite, which of the two—the merchant or the public official—is the less demanding parasite?

Business (I assume it to be free, or else what point would there be in my argument?) is forced, by its own self-interest, to study the seasons, to ascertain day by day the condition of the crops, to receive reports from all parts of the world, to foresee needs, to take precautions. It has ships all ready, associates everywhere, and its immediate self-interest is to buy at the lowest possible price, to economize on all details of operation, and to attain the greatest results with the least effort. Not only French merchants, but merchants the whole world over are busy with provisioning France for the day of need, and if self-interest compels them to fulfill their task at the least expense, competition among them no less compels them to let the consumers profit from all the economies realized. Once the wheat has arrived, the businessman has an interest in selling it as soon as possible to cover his risks, realize his profits, and begin all over again, if there is an opportunity. Guided by the comparison of prices, private enterprise distributes food all over the world, always beginning at the point of greatest scarcity, that is, where the need is felt the most. It is thus impossible to imagine an *organization* better calculated to serve the interests of the hungry, and the beauty of this organization, not perceived by the socialists, comes precisely from the fact that it is free, i.e., voluntary. True, the consumer must pay the businessman for his expenses of cartage, of transshipment, of storage, of commissions, etc., but under what system does the one who consumes the wheat avoid paying the expenses of shipping it to him? There is, besides, the necessity of paying also for *service rendered*, but, so far as the share of the middleman is concerned, it is reduced to a *minimum* by competition; and as to its justice, it would be strange for the artisans of Paris not to work for the merchants of Marseilles, when the merchants of Marseilles work for the artisans of Paris.

If, according to the socialist plan, the state takes the place of private businessmen in these transactions, what will happen? Pray, show me where there will be any economy for the public. Will it be in the retail price? But imagine the representatives of forty thousand municipalities arriving at Odessa on a given day, the day when the wheat is needed; imagine the effect on the price. Will the economy be effected in the shipping expenses? But will fewer ships, fewer sailors, fewer trans-shipments, fewer warehouses be needed, or are we to be relieved of the necessity for paying for all these things? Will the saving be effected in the profits of the businessmen? But did your representatives and public officials go to Odessa for nothing? Are they going to make the journey out of brotherly love? Will they not have to live? Will not their time have to be paid for? And do you think that this will not exceed a thousand times the two or three percent that the merchant earns, a rate that he is prepared to guarantee?

And then, think of the difficulty of levying so many taxes

to distribute so much food. Think of the injustices and abuses inseparable from such an enterprise. Think of the burden of responsibility that the government would have to bear.

The socialists who have invented these follies, and who in days of distress plant them in the minds of the masses, generously confer on themselves the title of "forward-looking" men, and there is a real danger that usage, that tyrant of language, will ratify both the word and the judgment it implies. "Forward-looking" assumes that these gentlemen can see ahead much further than ordinary people; that their only fault is to be too much in advance of their century; and that, if the time has not yet arrived when certain private services, allegedly parasitical, can be eliminated, the fault is with the public, which is far behind socialism. To *my* mind and knowledge, it is the contrary that is true, and I do not know to what barbaric century we should have to return to find on this point a level of understanding comparable to that of the socialists.

The modern socialist factions ceaselessly oppose free association in present-day society. They do not realize that a free society is a true association much superior to any of those that they concoct out of their fertile imaginations.

Let us elucidate this point with an example:

For a man, when he gets up in the morning, to be able to put on a suit of clothes, a piece of land has had to be enclosed, fertilized, drained, cultivated, planted with a certain kind of vegetation; flocks of sheep have had to feed on it; they have had to give their wool; this wool has had to be spun, woven, dyed, and converted into cloth; this cloth has had to be cut, sewn, and fashioned into a garment. And this series of operations implies a host of others; for it presupposes the use of farming implements, of sheepfolds, of factories, of coal, of machines, of carriages, etc.

If society were not a very real association, anyone who wanted a suit of clothes would be reduced to working in isolation, that is, to performing himself the innumerable operations in this series, from the first blow of the pickaxe that initiates it right down to the last thrust of the needle that terminates it.

But thanks to that readiness to associate which is the distinctive characteristic of our species, these operations have been distributed among a multitude of workers, and they keep subdividing themselves more and more for the common good to the point where, as consumption increases, a single specialized operation can support a new industry. Then comes the distribution of the proceeds, according to the portion of value each one has contributed to the total work. If this is not association, I should like to know what is.

Note that, since not one of the workers has produced the smallest particle of raw material from nothing, they are confined to rendering each other mutual services, to aiding each other for a common end; and that all can be considered, each group in relation to the others, as *middlemen*. If, for example, in the course of the operation, transportation becomes important enough to employ one person; spinning, a second; weaving, a third; why should the first one be considered more of a *parasite* than the others? Is there no need for transportation? Does not someone devote time and trouble to the task? Does he not spare his associates this time and trouble? Are they doing more than he, or just something different? Are they not all equally subject, in regard to their pay, that is, their share of the proceeds, to the law that restricts it to the *price agreed upon after bargaining*? Do not this division of labor and these arrangements, decided upon in full liberty, serve the common good? Do we, then, need a socialist, under the pretext of planning, to come and despotically destroy our voluntary arrangements, put an end to the division of labor, substitute isolated efforts for cooperative efforts, and reverse the progress of civilization?

Is association as I describe it here any the less association because everyone enters and leaves it voluntarily, chooses his place in it, judges and bargains for himself, under his own responsibility, and brings to it the force and the assurance of his own self-interest? For association to deserve the name, does a so-called reformer have to come and impose his formula and his will on us and concentrate within himself, so to speak, all of mankind?

The more one examines these "forward-looking" schools of thought, the more one is convinced that at bottom they rest on nothing but ignorance proclaiming itself infallible and demanding despotic power in the name of this infallibility.

I hope that the reader will excuse this digression. It is perhaps not entirely useless at the moment when, coming straight from the books of the Saint-Simonians, of the advocates of phalansteries, and of the admirers of Icaria, tirades against the middlemen fill the press and the Assembly and seriously menace the freedom of labor and exchange.

7. Restraint of Trade

Mr. Protectionist (it was not I who gave him that name; it was M. Charles Dupin) devoted his time and his capital to converting ore from his lands into iron. Since Nature had been more generous with the Belgians, they sold iron to the French at a better price than Mr. Protectionist did, which meant that all Frenchmen, or France, could obtain a given quantity of iron *with less labor* by buying it from the good people of Flanders. Therefore, prompted by their self-interest, they took full advantage of the situation, and every day a multitude of nailmakers, metalworkers, cartwrights, mechanics, blacksmiths, and plowmen could be seen either going themselves or sending middlemen to Belgium to obtain their supply of iron. Mr. Protectionist did not like this at all.

His first idea was to stop this abuse by direct intervention with his own two hands. This was certainly the least he could do, since he alone was harmed. I'll take my carbine, he said to himself. I'll put four pistols in my belt, I'll fill my cartridge box, I'll buckle on my sword, and, thus equipped, I'll go to the frontier. There I'll kill the first metalworker, nailmaker, blacksmith, mechanic, or locksmith who comes seeking his own profit rather than mine. That'll teach him a lesson!

At the moment of leaving, Mr. Protectionist had a few second thoughts that somewhat tempered his bellicose ardor. He said to himself: First of all, it is quite possible that the buyers of iron, my fellow countrymen and my enemies, will take offense, and, instead of letting themselves be killed, they might kill me. Furthermore, even if all my servants marched out, we could not guard the whole frontier. Finally, the entire proceeding would cost me too much, more than the result would be worth.

Mr. Protectionist was going to resign himself sadly just to being free like everyone else, when suddenly he had a brilliant idea.

He remembered that there is a great law factory in Paris. What is a law? he asked himself. It is a measure to which, when once promulgated, whether it is good or bad, everyone has to conform. For the execution of this law, a public police force is organized, and to make up the said public police force, men and money are taken from the nation.

If, then, I manage to get from that great Parisian factory a nice little law saying: "Belgian iron is prohibited," I shall attain the following results: The government will replace the few servants that I wanted to send to the frontier with twenty thousand sons of my recalcitrant metalworkers, locksmiths, nailmakers, blacksmiths, artisans, mechanics, and plowmen. Then, to keep these twenty thousand customs officers in good spirits and health, there will be distributed to them twenty-five million francs taken from these same blacksmiths, nailmakers, artisans, and plowmen. Organized in this way, the protection will be better accomplished; it will cost me nothing; I shall not be exposed to the brutality of brokers; I shall sell the iron at my price; and I shall enjoy the sweet pleasure of seeing our great people shamefully hoaxed. That will teach them to be continually proclaiming themselves the precursors and the promoters of all progress in Europe. It will be a smart move, and well worth the trouble of trying!

So Mr. Protectionist went to the law factory. (Another time, perhaps, I shall tell the story of his dark, underhanded dealings there; today I wish to speak only of the steps he took openly and for all to see.) He presented to their excellencies, the legislators, the following argument:

"Belgian iron is sold in France at ten francs, which forces me to sell mine at the same price. I should prefer to sell it at fifteen and cannot because of this confounded Belgian iron. Manufacture a law that says: 'Belgian iron shall no longer enter France.' Immediately I shall raise my price by five francs, with the following consequences:

"For each hundred kilograms of iron that I shall deliver to the public, instead of ten francs I shall get fifteen; I shall enrich myself more quickly; I shall extend the exploitation of my mines; I shall employ more men. My employees and I will spend more, to the great advantage of our suppliers for miles around. These suppliers, having a greater market, will give more orders to industry, and gradually this activity will spread throughout the country. This lucky hundred-sou piece that you will drop into my coffers, like a stone that is thrown into a lake, will cause an infinite number of concentric circles to radiate great distances in every direction."

Charmed by this discourse, enchanted to learn that it is so easy to increase the wealth of a people simply by legislation, the manufacturers of laws voted in favor of the restriction. "What is all this talk about labor and saving?" they said. "What good are these painful means of increasing the national wealth, when a decree will do the job?"

And, in fact, the law had all the consequences predicted by Mr. Protectionist, but it had others too; for, to do him justice, he had not reasoned *falsely,* but *incompletely.* In asking for a privilege, he had pointed out the effects *that are seen,* leaving in the shadow those *that are not seen.* He had shown only two people, when actually there are three in the picture. It is for us to repair this omission, whether involuntary or premeditated.

Yes, the five-franc piece thus legislatively rechanneled into the coffers of Mr. Protectionist constitutes an advantage for him and for those who get jobs because of it. And if the decree had made the five-franc piece come down from the moon, these good effects would not be counterbalanced by any compensating bad effects. Unfortunately, the mysterious hundred sous did not come down from the moon, but rather from the pocket of a metalworker, a nail-maker, a cartwright, a blacksmith, a plowman, a builder, in a word, from James Goodfellow, who pays it out today without receiving a milligram of iron more than when he was paying ten francs. It at once becomes evident that this certainly changes the question, for, quite obviously, the *profit* of Mr. Protectionist is counterbalanced by the *loss* of James Goodfellow, and anything that Mr. Protectionist will be able to do with this five-franc piece for the encouragement of domestic industry, James Goodfellow could also have done. The stone is thrown in at one point in the lake only because it has been prohibited by law from being thrown in at another.

Hence, *what is not seen* counterbalances *what is seen*; and the outcome of the whole operation is an injustice, all the more deplorable in having been perpetrated by the law.

But this is not all. I have said that a third person was always left in the shadow. I must make him appear here, so that he can reveal to us a *second loss* of five francs. Then we shall have the results of the operation in its entirety.

James Goodfellow has fifteen francs, the fruit of his labors. (We are back at the time when he is still free.) What does he do with his fifteen francs? He buys an article of millinery for ten francs, and it is with this article of millinery that he pays (or his middleman pays for him) for the hundred kilograms of Belgian iron. He still has five francs left. He does not throw them into the river, but (and this is *what is not seen*) he gives them to some manufacturer or other in exchange for some satisfaction—for example, to a publisher for a copy of the *Discourse on Universal History by Bossuet*.

Thus, he has encouraged *domestic industry* to the amount of fifteen francs, to wit:

10 francs to the Parisian milliner
5 francs to the publisher

And as for James Goodfellow, he gets for his fifteen francs two objects of satisfaction, to wit:

1. A hundred kilograms of iron
2. A book

Comes the decree.

What happens to James Goodfellow? What happens to domestic industry?

James Goodfellow, in giving his fifteen francs to the last centime to Mr. Protectionist for a hundred kilograms of iron, has nothing now but the use of this iron. He loses the enjoyment of a book or of any other equivalent object. He loses five francs. You agree with this; you cannot fail to agree; you cannot fail to agree that when restraint of trade raises prices, the consumer loses the difference.

But it is said that *domestic industry* gains the difference.

No, it does not gain it; for, since the decree, it is encouraged only as much as it was before, to the amount of fifteen francs.

Only, since the decree, the fifteen francs of James Goodfellow go to metallurgy, while before the decree they were divided between millinery and publishing.

The force that Mr. Protectionist might exercise by himself at the frontier and that which he has the law exercise for him can be judged quite differently from the moral point of view. There are people who think that plunder loses all its immorality as soon as it becomes legal. Personally, I cannot imagine a more alarming situation. However that may be, one thing is certain, and that is that the economic results are the same.

You may look at the question from any point of view you like, but if you examine it dispassionately, you will see that no good can come from legal or illegal plunder. We do not deny that it may bring for Mr. Protectionist or his industry, or if you wish for domestic industry, a profit of five francs. But we affirm that it will also give rise to two losses: one for James Goodfellow, who pays fifteen francs for what he used to get for ten, the other for domestic industry, which no longer receives the difference. Make your own choice of which of these two losses compensates for the profit that we admit. The one you do not choose constitutes no less a *dead loss*.

Moral: To use force is not to produce, but to destroy. Heavens! If to use force were to produce, France would be much richer than she is.

8. Machines

"A curse on machines! Every year their increasing power condemns to pauperism millions of workers, taking their jobs away from them, and with their jobs their wages, and with their wages their bread! A curse on machines!"

That is the cry rising from ignorant prejudice, and whose echo resounds in the newspapers.

But to curse machines is to curse the human mind!

What puzzles me is that it is possible to find anyone at all who can be content with such a doctrine.

For, in the last analysis, if it is true, what is its strictly logical consequence? It is that activity, well-being, wealth, and happiness are possible only for stupid nations, mentally static, to whom God has not given the disastrous gift of thinking, observing, contriving, inventing, obtaining the greatest results with the least trouble. On the contrary, rags, miserable huts, poverty, and stagnation are the inevitable portion of every nation that looks for and finds in iron, fire, wind, electricity, magnetism, the laws of chemistry and mechanics—in a word, in the forces of Nature—an addition to its own resources, and it is indeed appropriate to say with Rousseau: "Every man who thinks is a depraved animal."

But this is not all. If this doctrine is true, and as all men think and invent—as all, in fact, from first to last, and at every minute of their existence, seek to make the forces of Nature cooperate with them, to do more with less, to reduce their own manual labor or that of those whom they pay, to attain the greatest possible sum of satisfactions with the least possible amount of work—we must conclude that all mankind is on the way to decadence, precisely because of this intelligent aspiration toward progress that seems to torment every one of its members.

Hence, it would have to be established statistically that the inhabitants of Lancaster, fleeing that machine-ridden country, go in search of employment to Ireland, where machines are unknown; and, historically, that the shadow of barbarism darkens the epochs of civilization, and that civilization flourishes in times of ignorance and barbarism.

Evidently there is in this mass of contradictions something that shocks us and warns us that the problem conceals an element essential to its solution that has not been sufficiently brought to light.

The whole mystery consists in this: Behind *what is seen* lies *what is not seen.* I am going to try to shed some light on it. My demonstration can be nothing but a repetition of the preceding one, for the problem is the same.

Men have a natural inclination, if they are not prevented by force, to go for a *bargain*—that is, for something that, for an equivalent satisfaction, spares them labor—whether this bargain comes to them from a capable *foreign producer* or from a capable *mechanical producer.*

The theoretical objection that is raised against this inclination is the same in both cases. In one as in the other, the reproach is made that it apparently makes for a scarcity of jobs. However, its actual effect is not to make jobs scarce, but to *free* men's labor for other jobs.

And that is why, in practice, the same obstacle—force—is set up against it in both cases. The legislator *prohibits* foreign competition and *forbids* mechanical competition. For what other means can there be to stifle an inclination natural to all men than to take away their freedom?

In many countries, it is true, the legislator strikes at only one of these types of competition and confines himself to grumbling about the other. This proves only that in these countries the legislator is inconsistent.

That should not surprise us. On a false path there is always inconsistency; if this were not so, mankind would be destroyed. We have never seen and never shall see a false principle carried out completely. I have said elsewhere: Absurdity is the limit of inconsistency. I should like to add: It is also its proof.

Let us go on with our demonstration; it will not be lengthy.

James Goodfellow had two francs that he let two workers earn.

But now suppose that he devises an arrangement of ropes and weights that will shorten the work by half.

Then he obtains the same satisfaction, saves a franc, and discharges a worker.

He discharges a worker: *that is what is seen.*

Seeing only this, people say: "See how misery follows civilization! See how freedom is fatal to equality! The human mind has made a conquest, and immediately another worker has forever fallen into the abyss of poverty. Perhaps James Goodfellow can still continue to have both men work for him, but he cannot give them more than ten sous each, for they will compete with one another and will offer their services at a lower rate. This is how the rich get richer and the poor become poorer. We must remake society."

A fine conclusion, and one worthy of the initial premise!

Fortunately, both premise and conclusion are false, because behind the half of the phenomenon *that is seen* is the other half *that is not seen.*

The franc saved by James Goodfellow and the necessary effects of this saving are not seen.

Since, as a result of his own invention, James Goodfellow no longer spends more than one franc for manual labor in the pursuit of a given satisfaction, he has another franc left over.

If, then, there is somewhere an idle worker who offers his labor on the market, there is also somewhere a capitalist who offers his idle franc. These two elements meet and combine.

And it is clear as day that between the supply of and the demand for labor, between the supply of and the demand for wages, the relationship has in no way changed.

The invention and the worker, paid with the first franc, now do the work previously accomplished by two workers.

The second worker, paid with the second franc, performs some new work.

What has then been changed in the world? There is one national satisfaction the more; in other words, the invention is a gratuitous conquest, a gratuitous profit for mankind.

From the form in which I have given my demonstration we could draw this conclusion:

"It is the capitalist who derives all the benefits flowing from the invention of machines. The laboring class, even though it suffers from them only temporarily, never profits from them, since, according to what you yourself say, they *reallocate* a portion of the nation's industry without *diminishing* it, it is true, but also without *increasing* it."

It is not within the province of this essay to answer all objections. Its only object is to combat an ignorant prejudice, very dangerous and extremely widespread. I wished to prove that a new machine, in making a certain number of workers available for jobs, *necessarily* makes available at the same time the money that pays them. These workers and this money get together eventually to produce something that was impossible to produce before the invention; from which it follows that *the final result of the invention is an increase in satisfactions with the same amount of labor.*

Who reaps this excess of satisfactions?

Yes, at first it is the capitalist, the inventor, the first one who uses the machine successfully, and this is the reward for his genius and daring. In this case, as we have just seen, he realizes a saving on the costs of production, which, no matter how it is spent (and it always is), gives employment to just as many hands as the machine has made idle.

But soon competition forces him to lower his selling price by the amount of this saving itself.

And then it is no longer the inventor who reaps the benefits of the invention; it is the buyer of the product, the consumer, the public, including the workers—in a word, it is mankind.

And *what is not seen* is that the saving, thus procured for all the consumers, forms a fund from which wages can be drawn, replacing what the machine has drained off.

Thus (taking up again the foregoing example), James Goodfellow obtains a product by spending two francs for wages.

Thanks to his invention, the manual labor now costs him only one franc.

As long as he sells the product at the same price, there is one worker the fewer employed in making this special product: *that is what is seen*; but there is one worker the more employed by the franc James Goodfellow has saved: *that is what is not seen*.

When, in the natural course of events, James Goodfellow is reduced to lowering by one franc the price of the product, he no longer realizes a saving; then he no longer releases a franc for national employment in new production. But whoever acquires it, i.e., mankind, takes his place. Whoever buys the product pays one franc less, saves a franc, and necessarily hands over this saving to the fund for wages; this is again *what is not seen*.

Another solution to this problem, one founded on the facts, has been advanced.

Some have said: "The machine reduces the expenses of production and lowers the price of the product. The lowering of the price stimulates an increase in consumption, which necessitates an increase in production, and, finally, the use of as many workers as before the invention—or more." In support of this argument they cite printing, spinning, the press, etc.

This demonstration is not scientific.

We should have to conclude from it that, if the consumption of the special product in question remains stationary or nearly so, the machine will be harmful to employment. This is not so.

Suppose that in a certain country all the men wear hats. If with a machine the price of hats can be reduced by half, it does not *necessarily* follow that twice as many hats will be bought.

Will it be said, in that case, that a part of the national labor force has been made idle? Yes, according to ignorant reasoning. No, according to mine; for, even though in that country no one were to buy a single extra hat, the entire fund for wages would nevertheless remain intact; whatever did not go to the hat industry would be found in the saving realized by all consumers and would go to pay wages for the whole of the labor force that the machine had rendered unnecessary and to stimulate a new development of all industries.

And this is, in fact, the way things happen. I have seen newspapers at 80 francs; now they sell for 48. This is a saving of 32 francs for the subscribers. It is not certain, at least it is not inevitable, that the 32 francs continue to go into journalism; but what is certain, what is inevitable, is that if they do not take this direction, they will take another. One franc will be used to buy more newspapers, another for more food, a third for better clothes, a fourth for better furniture.

Thus, all industries are interrelated. They form a vast network in which all the lines communicate by secret channels. What is saved in one profits all. What is important is to understand clearly that never, never are economies effected at the expense of jobs and wages.

9. Credit

At all times, but especially in the last few years, people have dreamt of universalizing wealth by universalizing credit.

I am sure I do not exaggerate in saying that since the February Revolution, the Paris presses have spewed forth more than ten thousand brochures extolling this solution of the *social problem*.

This solution, alas, has as its foundation merely an optical illusion, insofar as an illusion can serve as a foundation for anything.

These people begin by confusing hard money with products; then they confuse paper money with hard money; and it is from these two confusions that they profess to derive a fact.

In this question it is absolutely necessary to forget money, coins, bank notes, and the other media by which products pass from hand to hand, in order to see only the products themselves, which constitute the real substance of a loan.

For when a farmer borrows fifty francs to buy a plow, it is not actually the fifty francs that is lent to him; it is the plow.

And when a merchant borrows twenty thousand francs to buy a house, it is not the twenty thousand francs he owes; it is the house.

Money makes its appearance only to facilitate the arrangement among several parties.

Peter may not be disposed to lend his plow, but James may be willing to lend his money. What does William do then? He borrows the money from James, and with this money he buys the plow from Peter.

But actually nobody borrows money for the sake of the money itself. We borrow money to get products.

Now, in no country is it possible to transfer from one hand to another more products than there are.

Whatever the sum of hard money and bills that circulates, the borrowers taken together cannot get more plows, houses, tools, provisions, or raw materials than the total number of lenders can furnish.

For let us keep well in mind that every borrower presupposes a lender, that every borrowing implies a loan.

This much being granted, what good can credit institutions do? They can make it easier for borrowers and lenders to find one another and reach an understanding. But what they cannot do is to increase instantaneously the total number of objects borrowed and lent.

However, the credit organizations would have to do just this in order for the end of the social reformers to be attained, since these gentlemen aspire to nothing less than to give plows, houses, tools, provisions, and raw materials to everyone who wants them.

And how do they imagine they will do this?

By giving to loans the guarantee of the state.

Let us go more deeply into the matter, for there is something here that is *seen* and something that *is not seen*. Let us try to see both.

Suppose that there is only one plow in the world and that two farmers want it.

Peter is the owner of the only plow available in France. John and James wish to borrow it. John, with his honesty, his property, and his good name, offers guarantees. One *believes* in him; he has *credit*. James does not inspire confidence or at any rate seems less reliable. Naturally, Peter lends his plow to John.

But now, under socialist inspiration, the state intervenes and says to Peter: "Lend your plow to James. We will guarantee you reimbursement, and this guarantee is worth more than John's, for he is the only one responsible for himself, and we, though it is true we have nothing, dispose of the wealth of all the taxpayers; if necessary, we will pay back the principal and the interest with their money."

So Peter lends his plow to James; *this is what is seen.*

And the socialists congratulate themselves, saying, "See how our plan has succeeded. Thanks to the intervention of the state, poor James has a plow. He no longer has to spade by hand; he is on the way to making his fortune. It is a benefit for him and a profit for the nation as a whole."

Oh no, gentlemen, it is not a profit for the nation, for here is *what is not seen.*

It is not seen that the plow goes to James because it did not go to John.

It is not seen that if James pushes a plow instead of spading, John will be reduced to spading instead of plowing.

Consequently, what one would like to think of as an *additional* loan is only the *reallocation* of a loan.

Furthermore, *it is not seen* that this reallocation involves two profound injustices: injustice to John, who, after having merited and won *credit* by his honesty and his energy, sees himself deprived; injustice to the taxpayers, obligated to pay a debt that does not concern them.

Will it be said that the government offers to John the same opportunities it does to James? But since there is only one plow available, two cannot be lent. The argument always comes back to the statement that, thanks to the intervention of the state, more will be borrowed than can be lent, for the plow represents here the total of available capital.

True, I have reduced the operation to its simplest terms; but test by the same touchstone the most complicated governmental credit institutions, and you will be convinced that they can have but one result: to reallocate credit, not to *increase* it. In a given country and at a given time, there is only a certain sum of available capital, and it is all placed somewhere. By guaranteeing insolvent debtors, the state can certainly increase the number of borrowers, raise the rate of interest (all at the expense of the taxpayer), but it cannot increase the number of lenders and the total value of the loans.

Do not impute to me, however, a conclusion from which I beg Heaven to preserve me. I say that the law should not artificially encourage borrowing; but I do not say that it should hinder it artificially. If in our hypothetical system or elsewhere there should be obstacles to the diffusion and application of credit, let the law remove them; nothing could be better or more just. But that, along with liberty, is all that social reformers worthy of the name should ask of the law.

10. Algeria

Four orators are all trying to be heard in the Assembly. At first they speak all at once, then one after the other. What have they said? Very beautiful things, surely, about the power and grandeur of France, the necessity of sowing in order to reap, the brilliant future of our vast colony, the advantage of redistributing our *surplus* population, etc., etc.; masterpieces of eloquence, always ornamented with this conclusion:

"Vote fifty million francs (more or less) to build ports and roads in Algeria so that we can transport colonists there, build houses for them, and clear fields for them. If you do this, you will have lifted a burden from the shoulders of the French worker, encouraged employment in Africa, and increased trade in Marseilles. It would be all profit."

Yes, that is true, if we consider the said fifty million francs only from the moment when the state spends them, if we look at where they go, and not whence they come, if we take into account only the good that they will do after they leave the coffers of the tax collectors, and not the harm that has been brought about, or, beyond that, the good that has been prevented, by causing them to enter the government coffers in the first place. Yes, from this limited point of view, everything is profit. The house built in Barbary is *what is seen*; the port laid out in Barbary is *what is seen*; the jobs created in Barbary are *what is seen*; a certain reduction in the labor force in France is *what is seen*; great business activity in Marseilles, *still what is seen*.

But there is something else *that is not seen*. It is that the fifty millions spent by the state can no longer be spent as they would have been by the taxpayers. From all the benefits attributed to public spending we must deduct all the harm caused by preventing private spending—at least if we are not to go so far as to say that James Goodfellow would have done nothing with the five-franc pieces he had fairly earned and that the tax took away from him; an absurd assertion, for if he went to the trouble of earning them, it was because he hoped to have the satisfaction of using them. He would have had his garden fenced and can no longer do so; *this is what is not seen*. He would have had his field marled and can no longer do so: *this is what is not seen*. He would have added to his tools and can no longer do so: *this is what is not seen*. He would be better fed, better clothed; he would have had his sons better educated; he would have increased the dowry of his daughter; and he can no longer do so: *this is what is not seen*. He would have joined a mutual-aid society and can no longer do so: *this is what is not seen*. On the one hand, the satisfactions that have been taken away from him and the means of action that have been destroyed in his hands; on the other hand, the work of the ditchdigger, the carpenter, the blacksmith, the tailor, and the schoolmaster of his village which he would have encouraged and which is now nonexistent: *this is still what is not seen*.

Our citizens are counting a great deal on the future prosperity of Algeria; granted. But let them also calculate the paralysis that in the meantime will inevitably strike France. People show me business flourishing in Marseilles; but if it is transacted with the product of taxation, I shall, on the other hand, point out an equal amount of business destroyed in the rest of the country. They say: "A colonist transported to Barbary is relief for the population that remains in the country." I reply: "How can that be if, in transporting this colonist to Algeria, we have also transported two or three times the capital that would have kept him alive in France?"

The only end I have in view is to make the reader understand that, in all public spending, behind the apparent good there is an evil more difficult to discern. To the best of my ability, I should like to get my reader into the habit of seeing the one and the other and of taking account of both.

When a public expenditure is proposed, it must be examined on its own merits, apart from its allegedly beneficial effect in increasing the number of jobs available, for any improvement in this direction is illusory. What public spending does in this regard, private spending would have done to the same extent. Therefore, the employment issue is irrelevant.

It is not within the province of this essay to evaluate the intrinsic worth of the public expenditures devoted to Algeria.

But I cannot refrain from making one general observation. It is that a presumption of economic benefit is never appropriate for expenditures made by way of taxation. Why? Here is the reason.

In the first place, justice always suffers from it somewhat. Since James Goodfellow has sweated to earn his hundred-sou piece with some satisfaction in view, he is irritated, to say the least, that the tax intervenes to take this satisfaction away from him and give it to someone else. Now, certainly it is up to those who levy the tax to give some good reasons for it. We have seen that the state gives a detestable reason when it says: "With these hundred sous I am going to put some men to work," for James Goodfellow (as soon as he has seen the light) will not fail to respond: "Good Lord! With a hundred sous I could have put them to work myself."

Once this argument on the part of the state has been disposed of, the others present themselves in all their nakedness, and the debate between the public treasury and poor James is very much simplified. If the state says to him: "I shall take a hundred sous from you to pay the policemen who relieve you of the necessity for guarding your own security, to pave the street you traverse every day, to pay the magistrate who sees to it that your property and your liberty are respected, to feed the soldier who defends our frontiers," James Goodfellow will pay without saying a word, or I am greatly mistaken. But if the state says to him: "I shall take your hundred sous to give you one sou as a premium in case you have cultivated your field well, or to teach your son what you do not want him to learn, or to allow a cabinet minister to add a hundred-and-first dish to his dinner; I shall take them to build a cottage in Algeria, not to mention taking a hundred sous more to support a colonist there and another hundred sous to support a soldier to guard the colonist and another hundred sous to support a general to watch over the soldier, etc., etc.," it seems to me that I hear poor James cry out: "This legal system very strongly resembles the law of the jungle!" And as the state foresees the objection, what does it do? It confuses everything; it advances a detestable argument that ought not to have any influence on the question: it speaks of the effect of the hundred sous on employment; it points to the cook and to the tradesman who supplies the needs of the minister; it shows us a colonist, a soldier, a general, living on the five francs; it shows us, in short, *what is seen*. As long as James Goodfellow has not learned to put next to this *what is not seen*, he will be duped. That is why I am forced to teach him by loud and long repetition.

From the fact that public expenditures reallocate jobs without increasing them there results against such expenditures a second and grave objection. To reallocate jobs is to displace workers and to disturb the natural laws that govern the distribution of population over the earth. When fifty million francs are left to the taxpayers, since the latter are situated throughout the country, the money fosters employment in the forty thousand municipalities of France; it acts as a bond that holds each man to his native land; it is distributed to as many workers as possible and to all imaginable industries. Now, if the state, taking these fifty millions from the citizens, accumulates them and spends them at a given place, it will draw to this place a proportional quantity of labor it has transferred from other places, a corresponding number of expatriated workers, a floating population, declassed, and, I daresay, dangerous when the money is used up! But this is what happens (and here I return to my subject): this feverish activity, blown, so to speak, into a narrow space, attracts everyone's eye and is *what is seen;* the people applaud, marvel at the beauty and ease of the procedure, and demand its repetition and extension. *What is not seen* is that an equal number of jobs, probably more useful, have been prevented from being created in the rest of France.

11. Thrift and Luxury

It is not only in the matter of public expenditures that *what is seen* eclipses *what is not seen.* By leaving in the shadow half of the political economy, this phenomenon of the seen and the unseen induces a false moral standard. It leads nations to view their moral interests and their material interests as antagonistic. What could be more discouraging or more tragic? Observe:

There is no father of a family who does not take it as his duty to teach his children order, good management, economy, thrift, moderation in spending.

There is no religion that does not inveigh against ostentation and luxury. That is all well and good; but, on the other hand, what is more popular than these adages:

"To hoard is to dry up the veins of the people."

"The luxury of the great makes for the comfort of the little fellow."

"Prodigals ruin themselves, but they enrich the state."

"It is with the surplus of the rich that the bread of the poor is made."

Certainly there is a flagrant contradiction here between the moral idea and the economic idea. How many eminent men, after having pointed out this conflict, look upon it with equanimity! This is what I have never been able to understand; for it seems to me that one can experience nothing more painful than to see two opposing tendencies in the heart of man. Mankind will be degraded by the one extreme as well as by the other! If thrifty, it will fall into dire want; if prodigal, it will fall into moral bankruptcy!

Fortunately, these popular maxims represent thrift and luxury in a false light, taking account only of the immediate consequences *that are seen* and not of the more remote effects *that are not seen.* Let us try to rectify this incomplete view.

Mondor and his brother Ariste, having divided their paternal inheritance, each have an income of fifty thousand francs a year. Mondor practices philanthropy in the fashionable way. He is a spendthrift. He replaces his furniture several times a year, changes his carriages every month; people talk about the ingenious devices to which he resorts to get rid of his money faster; in brief, he makes the high livers of Balzac and Alexander Dumas look pale by comparison.

What a chorus of praises always surround him! "Tell us about Mondor! Long live Mondor! He is the benefactor of the working-man. He is the good angel of the people! It is true that he wallows in luxury; he splashes pedestrians with mud; his own dignity and human dignity in general suffer somewhat from it. . . . But what of it? If he does not make himself useful by his own labor, he does so by means of his wealth. He puts money into circulation. His courtyard is never empty of tradesmen who always leave satisfied. Don't people say that coins are round so that they can roll?"

Ariste has adopted a quite different plan of life. If he is not an egoist, he is at least an *individualist*; for he is rational in his spending, seeks only moderate and reasonable enjoyments, thinks of the future of his children; in a word, he *saves*.

And now I want you to hear what the crowd says about him!

"What good is this mean rich man, this penny-pincher? Undoubtedly there is something impressive and touching in the simplicity of his life; furthermore, he is humane, benevolent, and generous. But he *calculates*. He does not run through his whole income. His house is not always shining with lights and swarming with people. What gratitude do the carpetmakers, the coachmakers, the horse dealers, and the confectioners owe to him?"

These judgments, disastrous to morality, are founded on the fact that there is one thing that strikes the eye: the spending of the prodigal brother; and another thing that escapes the eye: the equal or even greater spending of the economical brother.

But things have been so admirably arranged by the divine Inventor of the social order that in this, as in everything, political economy and morality, far from clashing, are in harmony, so that the wisdom of Ariste is not only more worthy, but even more *profitable,* than the folly of Mondor.

And when I say more profitable, I do not mean only more profitable to Ariste, or even to society in general, but more profitable to present-day workers, to the industry of the age.

To prove this, it suffices to set before the mind's eye those hidden consequences of human actions that the bodily eye does not see.

Yes, the prodigality of Mondor has effects visible to all eyes: everyone can see his berlines, his landaus, his phaetons, the delicate paintings on his ceilings, his rich carpets, the splendor of his mansion. Everyone knows that he runs his thoroughbreds in the races. The dinners that he gives at his mansion in Paris fascinate the crowd on the boulevard, and people say to one another: "There's a fine fellow, who, far from saving any of his income, is probably making a hole in his capital." *This is what is seen.*

It is not as easy to see, from the viewpoint of the interest of the workers, what becomes of Ariste's income. If we trace it, however, we shall assure ourselves that all of it, *down to the last centime,* goes to give employment to the workers, just as certainly as the income of Mondor. There is only this difference: The foolish spending of Mondor is bound to decrease continually and to reach a necessary end; the wise spending of Ariste will go on increasing year by year.

And if this is the case, certainly the public interest is in accord with morality.

Ariste spends for himself and his house twenty thousand francs a year. If this does not suffice to make him happy, he does not deserve to be called wise. He is touched by the ills that weigh on the poor; he feels morally obligated to relieve them somewhat and devotes ten thousand francs to acts of charity. Among businessmen, manufacturers, and farmers he has friends who, for the moment, find themselves financially embarrassed. He inquires about their situation in order to come to their aid prudently and efficaciously and sets aside for this work another ten thousand francs. Finally, he does not forget that he has daughters to provide dowries for, sons to assure a future for, and, consequently, he imposes on himself the duty of saving and investing ten thousand francs a year.

This, then, is how he uses his income:

1. Personal expenses   20,000 francs
2. Charity   10,000 francs
3. Help to friends   10,000 francs
4. Savings   10,000 francs

If we review each of these items, we shall see that not a centime escapes going into the support of national industry.

1. *Personal expenses.* These, for workmen and shopkeepers, have effects absolutely identical to an equal amount spent by Mondor. This is self-evident; let us not discuss it further.

2. *Charity.* The ten thousand francs devoted to this end will support industry just as much; they will go to the baker, the butcher, the tailor, and the furniture dealer, except that the bread, the meat, the clothes do not serve the needs of Ariste directly, but of those whom he has substituted for himself. Now, this simple substitution of one consumer for another has no effect at all on industry in general. Whether Ariste spends a hundred sous or asks a poor person to spend it in his place is all one.

3. *Help to friends.* The friend to whom Ariste lends or gives ten thousand francs does not receive them in order to bury them; that would be contrary to our hypothesis. He uses them to pay for merchandise or to pay off his debts. In the first case, industry is encouraged. Will anyone dare say that there is more gained from Mondor's purchase of a thoroughbred for ten thousand francs than from a purchase by Ariste or his friends of ten thousand francs' worth of cloth? If this sum serves to pay a debt, all that results is that a third person appears, the creditor, who will handle the ten thousand francs, but who will certainly use them for something in his business, his factory, or his exploitation of natural resources. He is just one more intermediary between Ariste and the workers. The names change, the spending remains, and so does the encouragement of industry.

4. *Savings.* There remain the ten thousand francs *saved*; and it is here that, from the point of view of encouragement of the arts, industry, and the employment of workers, Mondor appears superior to Ariste, although morally Ariste shows himself a little superior to Mondor.

It is not without actual physical pain that I see such contradictions appear between the great laws of Nature. If mankind were reduced to choosing between the two sides, one of which hurts its interests and the other its conscience, we should have to despair for its future. Happily this is not so. To see Ariste regain his economic as well as his moral superiority, we need only understand this consoling axiom, which is not the less true for having a paradoxical appearance: *To save is to spend.*

What is Ariste's object in saving ten thousand francs? Is it to hide two thousand hundred-sou pieces in a hole in his garden? No, certainly not. He intends to increase his capital and his income. Consequently, this money that he does not use to buy personal satisfactions he uses to buy pieces of land, a house, government bonds, industrial enterprises; or perhaps he invests it with a broker or a banker. Follow the money through all these hypothetical uses, and you will be convinced that, through the intermediary of sellers or borrowers, it will go to support industry just as surely as if Ariste, following the example of his brother, had exchanged it for furniture, jewels, and horses.

For when Ariste buys for ten thousand francs pieces of land or bonds, he does so because he feels he does not need to spend this sum. This seems to be what you hold against him.

But, by the same token, the person who sells the piece of land or the mortgage is going to have to spend in some way the ten thousand francs he receives.

So that the spending is done in either case, whether by Ariste or by those who are substituted for him.

From the point of view of the working class and of the support given to industry, there is, then, only one difference between the conduct of Ariste and that of Mondor. The spending of Mondor is directly accomplished by him and around him; *it is seen.* That of Ariste, being carried out partly by intermediaries and at a distance, *is not seen.* But in fact, for anyone who can connect effects to their causes, that which is not seen is every bit as real as that which is seen. What proves it is that in both cases the money *circulates,* and that no more of it remains in the coffers of the wise brother than in those of the prodigal.

It is therefore false to say that thrift does actual harm to industry. In this respect it is just as beneficial as luxury.

But how superior it appears, if our thinking, instead of confining itself to the passing hour, embraces a long period of time!

Ten years have gone by. What has become of Mondor and his fortune and his great popularity? It has all vanished. Mondor is ruined; far from pouring fifty thousands francs into the economy every year, he is probably a public charge. In any case he is no longer the joy of the shopkeepers; he is no longer considered a promoter of the arts and of industry; he is no longer any good to the workers, nor to his descendants, whom he leaves in distress.

At the end of the same ten years Ariste not only continues to put all of his income into circulation, but he contributes increasing income from year to year. He adds to the national capital, that is to say, the funds that provide wages; and since the demand for workers depends on the extent of these funds, he contributes to the progressive increase of remuneration of the working class. Should he die, he will leave children who will replace him in this work of progress and civilization.

Morally, the superiority of thrift over luxury is incontestable. It is consoling to think that, from the economic point of view, it has the same superiority for whoever, not stopping at the immediate effects of things, can push his investigations to their ultimate effects.

12. The Right to Employment and the Right to Profit

"Brothers, assess yourselves to furnish me work at your price." This is the right to employment, elementary or first-degree socialism.

"Brothers, assess yourselves to furnish me work at my price." This is the right to profit, refined or second-degree socialism.

Both live by virtue of such of their effects *as are seen*. They will die from those of their effects *that are not seen*.

What is seen is the work and the profit stimulated by the assessments levied on society. *What is not seen* is the work and the profits that would come from this same amount of money if it were left in the hands of the taxpayers themselves.

In 1848 the right to employment showed itself for a moment with two faces. That was enough to ruin it in public opinion.

One of these faces was called: *National workshop*.

The other: *Forty-five centimes*.

Millions went everyday from the rue de Rivoli to the national workshops. This was the beautiful side of the coin.

But here is what was on the other side. In order for millions of francs to come out of a coffer, they must first have come into it.

That is why the organizers of the right to employment addressed themselves to the taxpayers.

Now, the farmers said: "I must pay forty-five centimes. Then I shall be deprived of clothes; I cannot marl my field; I cannot have my house repaired."

And the hired hands said: "Since our boss is not going to have any new clothes, there will be less work for the tailor; since he is not going to have his field marled, there will be less work for the ditchdigger; since he is not going to have his house repaired, there will be less work for the carpenter and the mason."

It was therefore proved that you cannot profit twice from the same transaction, and that the work paid for by the government was created at the expense of work that would have been paid for by the taxpayer. That was the end of the right to employment, which came to be seen as an illusion as well as an injustice.

However, the right to profit, which is nothing but an exaggeration of the right to employment, is still alive and flourishing.

Is there not something shameful in the role that the protectionist makes society play?

He says to society:

"You must give me work, and, what is more, lucrative work. I have foolishly chosen an industry that leaves me with a loss of ten percent. If you slap a tax of twenty francs on my fellow citizens and excuse me from paying it, my loss will be converted into a profit. Now, profit is a right; you owe it to me."

The society that listens to this sophist, that will levy taxes on itself to satisfy him, that does not perceive that the loss wiped out in one industry is no less a loss because others are forced to shoulder it—this society, I say, deserves the burden placed upon it.

Thus, we see, from the many subjects I have dealt with, that not to know political economy is to allow oneself to be dazzled by the immediate effect of a phenomenon; to know political economy is to take into account the sum total of all effects, both immediate and future.

I could submit here a host of other questions to the same test. But I desist from doing so, because of the monotony of demonstrations that would always be the same, and I conclude by applying to political economy what Chateaubriand said of history:

There are two consequences in history: one immediate and instantaneously recognized; the other distant and unperceived at first. These consequences often contradict each other; the former come from our short-run wisdom, the latter from long-run wisdom. The providential event appears after the human event. Behind men rises God. Deny as much as you wish the Supreme Wisdom, do not believe in its action, dispute over words, call what the common man calls Providence "the force of circumstances" or "reason"; but look at the end of an accomplished fact, and you will see that it has always produced the opposite of what was expected when it has not been founded from the first on morality and justice.

(Chateaubriand, *Memoirs from beyond the Tomb*.)

A Petition

by Frédéric Bastiat

From the Manufacturers of Candles, Tapers, Lanterns, Candlesticks, Street Lamps, Snuffers, and Extinguishers, and from the Producers of Tallow, Oil, Resin, Alcohol, and Generally of Everything Connected with Lighting.

To the Honorable Members of the Chamber of Deputies.

 Gentlemen:

You are on the right track. You reject abstract theories and have little regard for abundance and low prices. You concern yourselves mainly with the fate of the producer. You wish to free him from foreign competition, that is, to reserve the *domestic market* for *domestic industry*.

We come to offer you a wonderful opportunity for applying your—what shall we call it? Your theory? No, nothing is more deceptive than theory. Your doctrine? Your system? Your principle? But you dislike doctrines, you have a horror of systems, and, as for principles, you deny that there are any in political economy; therefore we shall call it your practice—your practice without theory and without principle.

We are suffering from the ruinous competition of a foreign rival who apparently works under conditions so far superior to our own for the production of light that he is *flooding* the *domestic market* with it at an incredibly low price; for the moment he appears, our sales cease, all the consumers turn to him, and a branch of French industry whose ramifications are innumerable is all at once reduced to complete stagnation. This rival, which is none other than the sun, is waging war on us so mercilessly that we suspect he is being stirred up against us by perfidious Albion (excellent diplomacy nowadays!), particularly because he has for that haughty island a respect that he does not show for us.

We ask you to be so good as to pass a law requiring the closing of all windows, dormers, skylights, inside and outside shutters, curtains, casements, bull's-eyes, deadlights, and blinds—in short, all openings, holes, chinks, and fissures through which the light of the sun is wont to enter houses, to the detriment of the fair industries with which, we are proud to say, we have endowed the country, a country that cannot, without betraying ingratitude, abandon us today to so unequal a combat.

Be good enough, honorable deputies, to take our request seriously, and do not reject it without at least hearing the reasons that we have to advance in its support.

First, if you shut off as much as possible all access to natural light, and thereby create a need for artificial light, what industry in France will not ultimately be encouraged?

If France consumes more tallow, there will have to be more cattle and sheep, and, consequently, we shall see an increase in cleared fields, meat, wool, leather, and especially manure, the basis of all agricultural wealth.

If France consumes more oil, we shall see an expansion in the cultivation of the poppy, the olive, and rapeseed. These rich yet soil-exhausting plants will come at just the right time to enable us to put to profitable use the increased fertility that the breeding of cattle will impart to the land.

Our moors will be covered with resinous trees. Numerous swarms of bees will gather from our mountains the perfumed treasures that today waste their fragrance, like the flowers from which they emanate. Thus, there is not one branch of agriculture that would not undergo a great expansion.

The same holds true of shipping. Thousands of vessels will engage in whaling, and in a short time we shall have a fleet capable of upholding the honor of France and of gratifying the patriotic aspirations of the undersigned petitioners, chandlers, etc.

But what shall we say of the *specialties of Parisian manufacture*? Henceforth you will behold gilding, bronze, and crystal in candlesticks, in lamps, in chandeliers, in candelabra sparkling in spacious emporia compared with which those of today are but stalls.

There is no needy resin-collector on the heights of his sand dunes, no poor miner in the depths of his black pit, who will not receive higher wages and enjoy increased prosperity.

It needs but a little reflection, gentlemen, to be convinced that there is perhaps not one Frenchman, from the wealthy stockholder of the Anzin Company to the humblest vendor of matches, whose condition would not be improved by the success of our petition.

We anticipate your objections, gentlemen; but there is not a single one of them that you have not picked up from the musty old books of the advocates of free trade. We defy you to utter a word against us that will not instantly rebound against yourselves and the principle that guides your entire policy.

Will you tell us that, though we may gain by this protection, France will not gain at all, because the consumer will bear the expense?

We have our answer ready:

You no longer have the right to invoke the interests of the consumer. You have sacrificed him whenever you have found his interests opposed to those of the producer. You have done so in order *to encourage industry and to increase employment.* For the same reason you ought to do so this time too.

Indeed, you yourselves have anticipated this objection. When told that the consumer has a stake in the free entry of iron, coal, sesame, wheat, and textiles, "Yes," you reply, "but the producer has a stake in their exclusion." Very well! Surely if consumers have a stake in the admission of natural light, producers have a stake in its interdiction.

"But," you may still say, "the producer and the consumer are one and the same person. If the manufacturer profits by protection, he will make the farmer prosperous. Contrariwise, if agriculture is prosperous, it will open markets for manufactured goods." Very well! If you grant us a monopoly over the production of lighting during the day, first of all we shall buy large amounts of tallow, charcoal, oil, resin, wax, alcohol, silver, iron, bronze, and crystal, to supply our industry; and, moreover, we and our numerous suppliers, having become rich, will consume a great deal and spread prosperity into all areas of domestic industry.

Will you say that the light of the sun is a gratuitous gift of Nature, and that to reject such gifts would be to reject wealth itself under the pretext of encouraging the means of acquiring it?

But if you take this position, you strike a mortal blow at your own policy; remember that up to now you have always excluded foreign goods *because* and *in proportion as* they approximate gratuitous gifts. You have only *half* as good a reason for complying with the demands of other monopolists as you have for granting our petition, which is in *complete* accord with your established policy; and to reject our demands precisely because they are *better founded* than anyone else's would be tantamount to accepting the equation: $+ ? = + -$; in other words, it would be to heap *absurdity* upon *absurdity*.

Labor and Nature collaborate in varying proportions, depending upon the country and the climate, in the production of a commodity. The part that Nature contributes is always free of charge; it is the part contributed by human labor that constitutes value and is paid for.

If an orange from Lisbon sells for half the price of an orange from Paris, it is because the natural heat of the sun, which is, of course, free of charge, does for the former what the latter owes to artificial heating, which necessarily has to be paid for in the market.

Thus, when an orange reaches us from Portugal, one can say that it is given to us half free of charge, or, in other words, at *half price* as compared with those from Paris.

Now, it is precisely on the basis of its being *semigratuitous* (pardon the word) that you maintain it should be barred. You ask: "How can French labor withstand the competition of foreign labor when the former has to do all the work, whereas the latter has to do only half, the sun taking care of the rest?" But if the fact that a product is *half* free of charge leads you to exclude it from competition, how can its being *totally* free of charge induce you to admit it into competition? Either you are not consistent, or you should, after excluding what is half free of charge as harmful to our domestic industry, exclude what is totally gratuitous with all the more reason and with twice the zeal.

To take another example: When a product—coal, iron, wheat, or textiles—comes to us from abroad, and when we can acquire it for less labor than if we produced it ourselves, the difference is a *gratuitous gift* that is conferred upon us. The size of this gift is proportionate to the extent of this difference. It is a quarter, a half, or three-quarters of the value of the product if the foreigner asks of us only three-quarters, one-half, or one-quarter as high a price. It is as complete as it can be when the donor, like the sun in providing us with light, asks nothing from us. The question, and we pose it formally, is whether what you desire for France is the benefit of consumption free of charge or the alleged advantages of onerous production. Make your choice, but be logical; for as long as you ban, as you do, foreign coal, iron, wheat, and textiles, *in proportion* as their price approaches *zero,* how inconsistent it would be to admit the light of the sun, whose price is zero all day long!

A Negative Railroad

by Frédéric Bastiat

I have said that as long as one has regard, as unfortunately happens, only to the interest of the producer, it is impossible to avoid running counter to the general interest, since the producer, as such, demands nothing but the multiplication of obstacles, wants, and efforts.

I find a remarkable illustration of this in a Bordeaux newspaper.

M. Simiot raises the following question:

Should there be a break in the tracks at Bordeaux on the railroad from Paris to Spain?

He answers the question in the affirmative and offers a number of reasons, of which I propose to examine only this:

There should be a break in the railroad from Paris to Bayonne at Bordeaux; for, if goods and passengers are forced to stop at that city, this will be profitable for boatmen, porters, owners of hotels, etc.

Here again we see clearly how the interests of those who perform services are given priority over the interests of the consumers.

But if Bordeaux has a right to profit from a break in the tracks, and if this profit is consistent with the public interest, then Angoulême, Poitiers, Tours, Orléans, and, in fact, all the intermediate points, including Ruffec, Châtellerault, etc., etc., ought also to demand breaks in the tracks, on the ground of the general interest—in the interest, that is, of domestic industry—for the more there are of these breaks in the line, the greater will be the amount paid for storage, porters, and cartage at every point along the way. By this means, we shall end by having a railroad composed of a whole series of breaks in the tracks, i.e., a *negative railroad*.

Whatever the protectionists may say, it is no less certain that the *basic principle of restriction* is the same as the *basic principle of breaks in the tracks:* the sacrifice of the consumer to the producer, of the end to the means.

The Balance of Trade

by Frédéric Bastiat

The balance of trade is an article of faith.

We know what it consists in: if a country imports more than it exports, it loses the difference. Conversely, if its exports exceed its imports, the excess is to its profit. This is held to be an axiom, and laws are passed in accordance with it.

On this hypothesis, M. Mauguin warned us the day before yesterday, citing statistics, that France carries on a foreign trade in which it has managed to lose, out of good will, without being required to do so, two hundred million francs a year.

"You have lost by your trade, in eleven years, two billion francs. Do you understand what that means?"

Then, applying his infallible rule to the facts, he told us: "In 1847 you sold 605 million francs' worth of manufactured products, and you bought only 152 millions' worth. Hence, you *gained* 450 million.

"You bought 804 millions' worth of raw materials, and you sold only 114 million; hence, you *lost* 690 million."

This is an example of the dauntless naïveté of following an absurd premise to its logical conclusion. M. Mauguin has discovered the secret of making even Messrs. Darblay and Lebeuf laugh at the expense of the balance of trade. It is a great achievement, of which I cannot help being jealous.

Allow me to assess the validity of the rule according to which M. Mauguin and all the protectionists calculate profits and losses. I shall do so by recounting two business transactions which I have had the occasion to engage in.

I was at Bordeaux. I had a cask of wine which was worth 50 francs; I sent it to Liverpool, and the customhouse noted on its records an *export* of 50 francs.

At Liverpool the wine was sold for 70 francs. My representative converted the 70 francs into coal, which was found to be worth

53

90 francs on the market at Bordeaux. The customhouse hastened to record an *import* of 90 francs.

Balance of trade, or the excess of imports over exports: 40 francs.

These 40 francs, I have always believed, putting my trust in my books, I had gained. But M. Mauguin tells me that I have lost them, and that France has lost them in my person.

And why does M. Mauguin see a loss here? Because he supposes that any excess of imports over exports necessarily implies a balance that must be paid in cash. But where is there in the transaction that I speak of, which follows the pattern of all profitable commercial transactions, any balance to pay? Is it, then, so difficult to understand that a merchant compares the prices current in different markets and decides to trade only when he has the certainty, or at least the probability, of seeing the exported value return to him increased? Hence, what M. Mauguin calls *loss* should be called *profit*.

A few days after my transaction I had the simplicity to experience regret; I was sorry I had not waited. In fact, the price of wine fell at Bordeaux and rose at Liverpool; so that if I had not been so hasty, I could have bought at 40 francs and sold at 100 francs. I truly believed that on such a basis my *profit* would have been greater. But I learn from M. Mauguin that it is the *loss* that would have been more ruinous.

My second transaction had a very different result.

I had had some truffles shipped from Périgord which cost me 100 francs; they were destined for two distinguished English cabinet ministers for a very high price, which I proposed to turn into pounds sterling. Alas, I would have done better to eat them myself (I mean the truffles, not the English pounds or the Tories). All would not have been lost, as they were, for the ship that carried them off sank on its departure. The customs officer, who had noted on this occasion an export of 100 francs, never had any re-import to enter in this case.

Hence, M. Mauguin would say, France gained 100 francs; for it was, in fact, by this sum that the export, thanks to the shipwreck, exceeded the import. If the affair had turned out otherwise, if I had received 200 or 300 francs' worth of English pounds, then the balance of trade would have been unfavorable, and France would have been the loser.

From the point of view of science, it is sad to think that all the commercial transactions which end in loss according to the businessmen concerned show a profit according to that class of theorists who are always declaiming against theory.

But from the point of view of practical affairs, it is even sadder, for what is the result?

Suppose that M. Mauguin had the power (and to a certain extent he has, by his votes) to substitute his calculations and desires for the calculations and desires of businessmen and to give, in his words, "a good commercial and industrial organization to the country, a good impetus to domestic industry." What would he do?

M. Mauguin would suppress by law all transactions that consist in buying at a low domestic price in order to sell at a high price abroad and in converting the proceeds into commodities eagerly sought after at home; for it is precisely in these transactions that the imported value exceeds the exported value.

Conversely, he would tolerate, and, indeed, he would encourage, if necessary by subsidies (from taxes on the public), all enterprises based on the idea of buying dearly in France in order to sell cheaply abroad; in other words, exporting what is useful to us in order to import what is useless. Thus, he would leave us perfectly free, for example, to send off cheeses from Paris to Amsterdam, in order to bring back the latest fashions from Amsterdam to Paris; for in this traffic the balance of trade would always be in our favor.

Yet, it is sad and, I dare add, degrading that the legislator will not let the interested parties decide and act for themselves in these matters, at their peril and risk. At least then everyone bears the responsibility for his own acts; he who makes a mistake is punished and is set right. But when the legislator imposes and prohibits, should he make a monstrous error in judgment, that error must become the rule of conduct for the whole of a great nation. In France we love freedom very much, but we hardly understand it. Oh, let us try to understand it better! We shall not love it any the less.

M. Mauguin has stated with imperturbable aplomb that there is not a statesman in England who does not accept the doctrine of the balance of trade. After having calculated the loss which, according to him, results from the excess of our imports, he cried out: "If a similar picture were to be presented to the English, they would shudder, and there is not a member in the House of Commons who would not feel that his seat was threatened."

For my part, I affirm that if someone were to say to the House of Commons: "The total value of what is exported from the country exceeds the total value of what is imported," it is then that they would feel threatened; and I doubt that a single speaker could be found who would dare to add: "The difference represents a profit."

In England they are convinced that it is important for the nation to receive more than it gives. Moreover, they have observed that this is the attitude of all businessmen; and that is why they have taken the side of *laissez faire* and are committed to restoring free trade.

Twenty Myths about Markets

By Tom G. Palmer

When thinking about the merits and the limitations of solving problems of social coordination through market mechanisms, it's useful to clear away some common myths. By myths I mean those statements that simply pass for obviously true, without any need for argument or evidence. They're the kind of thing you hear on the radio, from friends, from politicians—they just seem to be in the air. They are repeated as if they're a kind of deeper wisdom. The danger is that, because they are so widespread, they are not subjected to critical examination. That is what I propose to do here.

Most, but not all, such myths are spread by those who are hostile to free markets.

A few are spread in much smaller circles by people who are perhaps too enthusiastic about free markets.

What follows are twenty such myths, grouped into four categories:

> Ethical Criticisms;
> Economic Criticisms;
> Hybrid Ethical-Economic Criticisms; and
> Overly Enthusiastic Defenses.

ETHICAL CRITICISMS

1. Markets Are Immoral or Amoral

Markets make people think only about the calculation of advantage, pure and simple. There's no morality in market exchange, no commitment to what makes us distinct as humans: our ability to think not only about what's advantageous to us, but about what is right and what is wrong, what is moral and what is immoral.

A more false claim would be hard to imagine. For there to be exchange there has to be respect for justice. People who exchange differ from people who merely take; exchangers show respect for the rightful claims of other people. The reason that people engage in exchange in the first place is that they want what others have but are constrained by morality and law from simply taking it. An exchange is a change from one allocation of resources to another; that means that any exchange is measured against a baseline, such that if no exchange takes place, the parties keep what they already have. The framework for exchange requires a sound foundation in justice. Without such moral and legal foundations, there can be no exchange.

Markets are not merely founded on respect for justice, however. They are also founded on the ability of humans to take into account, not only their own desires, but the desires of others, to put themselves in the places of others. A restaurateur who didn't care what his diners wanted would not be in business long. If the guests are made sick by the food, they won't come back. If the food fails to please them, they won't come back. He will be out of business. Markets provide incentives for participants to put themselves in the position of others, to consider what their desires are, and to try to see things as they see them.

Markets are the alternative to violence. Markets make us social. Markets remind us that other people matter, too.

2. Markets Promote Greed and Selfishness

People in markets are just trying to find the lowest prices or make the highest profits. As such, they're motivated only by greed and selfishness, not by concern for others.

Markets neither promote nor dampen selfishness or greed. They make it possible for the most altruistic, as well as the most selfish, to advance their purposes in peace. Those who dedicate their lives to helping others use markets to advance their purposes, no less than those whose goal is to increase their store of wealth. Some of the latter even accumulate wealth for the purpose of increasing their ability to help others. George Soros and Bill Gates are examples of the latter; they earn huge amounts of money, at least partly in order to increase their ability to help others through their vast charitable activities.

A Mother Teresa wants to use the wealth available to her to feed, clothe, and comfort the greatest number of people. Markets allow her to find the lowest prices for blankets, for food, and for medicines to care for those who need her assistance. Markets allow the creation of wealth that can be used to help the unfortunate and facilitate the charitable to maximize their ability to help others. Markets make possible the charity of the charitable.

A common mistake is to identify the purposes of people with their "self-interest," which is then in turn confused with "selfishness." The purposes of people in the market are indeed purposes of selves, but as selves with purposes we are also concerned about the interests and well-being of others—our family members, our friends, our neighbors, and even total strangers whom we will never meet. And as noted above, markets help to condition people to consider the needs of others, including total strangers.

As has often been pointed out, the deepest foundation of human society is not love or even friendship. Love and friendship are the fruits of mutual benefit through cooperation, whether in small or in large groups. Without such mutual benefit, society would simply be impossible. Without the possibility of mutual benefit, Tom's good would be June's bad, and vice versa, and they could never be cooperators, never be colleagues, never be friends. Cooperation is tremendously enhanced by markets, which allow cooperation even among those who are not personally known to each other, who don't share the same religion or language, and who may never meet. The existence of potential gains from trade and the facilitation of trade by well-defined and legally secure property rights make possible charity among strangers, and love and friendship across borders.

3. Reliance on Markets Leads to Monopoly

Without government intervention, reliance on free markets would lead to a few big firms selling everything. Markets naturally create monopolies, as marginal producers are squeezed out by firms that seek nothing but their own profits, whereas governments are motivated to seek the public interest and will act to restrain monopolies.

Governments can—and all too often do—give monopolies to favored individuals or groups; that is, they prohibit others from entering the market and competing for the custom of customers. That's what a monopoly means. The monopoly may be granted to a government agency itself (as in the monopolized postal services in many countries) or it may be granted to a favored firm, family, or person.

Do free markets promote monopolization? There's little or no good reason to think so and many reasons to think not. Free markets rest on the freedom of persons to enter the market, to exit the market, and to buy from or sell to whomever they please. If firms in markets with freedom of entry make above average profits, those profits attract rivals to compete those profits away. Some of the literature of economics offers descriptions of hypothetical situations in which certain market conditions *could* lead to persistent "rents," that is, income in excess of opportunity cost, defined as what the resources could earn in other uses. But concrete examples are extremely hard to find, other than relatively uninteresting cases such as ownership of unique resources (for example, a painting by Rembrandt). In contrast, the historical record is simply full of examples of governments granting special privileges to their supporters.

Freedom to enter the market and freedom to choose from whom to buy promote consumer interests by eroding those temporary rents that the first to offer a good or service may enjoy. In contrast, endowing governments with power to determine who may or may not provide goods and services creates the monopolies—the actual, historically observed monopolies—that are harmful to consumers and that restrain the productive forces of mankind on which human betterment rests. If markets routinely led to monopolies, we would not expect to see so many people going to government to grant them monopolies at the expense of their less powerful competitors and customers. They could get their monopolies through the market, instead.

It's always worth remembering that government itself seeks to exercise a monopoly; it's a classic defining characteristic of a government that it exercises a monopoly on the exercise of force in a given geographic area. Why should we expect such a monopoly to be more friendly to competition than the market itself, which is defined by the freedom to compete?

4. Markets Depend on Perfect Information, Requiring Government Regulation to Make Information Available

For markets to be efficient, all market participants have to be fully informed of the costs of their actions. If some have more information than others, such asymmetries will lead to inefficient and unjust outcomes. Government has to intervene to provide the information that markets lack and to create outcomes that are both efficient and just.

Information, like every other thing we want, is always costly, that is, we have to give something up to get more of it. Information is itself a product that is exchanged on markets; for example, we buy books that contain information because we value the information in the book more than we value what we give up for it. Markets do not require for their operation perfect information, any more than democracies do. The assumption that information is costly to market participants but costless to political participants is unrealistic in extremely destructive ways. Neither politicians nor voters have perfect information. Significantly, politicians and voters have less incentive to acquire the right amount of information than do market participants, because they aren't spending their own money. For example, when spending money from the public purse, politicians don't have the incentive to be as careful or to acquire as much information as people do when they are spending their own money.

A common argument for state intervention rests on the informational asymmetries between consumers and providers of specialized services. Doctors are almost always more knowledgeable about medical matters than are patients, for example; that's why we go to doctors, rather than just curing ourselves. Because of that, it is alleged that consumers have no way of knowing which doctors are more competent, or whether they are getting the right treatment, or whether they are paying too much. Licensing by the state may then be proposed as the answer; by issuing a license, it is sometimes said, people are assured that the doctor will be qualified, competent, and upright. The evidence from studies of licensure, of medicine and of other professions, however, shows quite the opposite. Whereas markets tend to generate gradations of certification, licensing is binary; you are licensed, or you are not. Moreover, it's common in licensed professions that the license is revoked if the licensed professional engages in "unprofessional conduct," which is usually defined as including advertising! But advertising is one of the means that markets have evolved to provide information—about the availability of products and services, about relative qualities, and about prices. Licensure is not the solution to cases of informational asymmetry; it is the cause.

5. Markets Only Work When an Infinite Number of People With Perfect Information Trade Undifferentiated Commodities

Market efficiency, in which output is maximized and profits are minimized, requires that no one is a price-setter, that is, that no buyer or seller, by entering or exiting the market, will affect the price. In a perfectly competitive market, no individual buyer or seller can have any impact on prices. Products are all homogenous and information about products and prices is costless. But real markets are not perfectly competitive, which is why government is required to step in and correct things.

Abstract models of economic interaction can be useful, but when normatively loaded terms such as "perfect" are added to theoretical abstractions, a great deal of harm can be done. If a certain condition of the market is defined as "perfect" competition, then anything else is "imperfect" and needs to be improved, presumably by some agency outside of the market. In fact, "perfect" competition is simply a mental model, from which we can deduce certain interesting facts, such as the role of profits in directing resources (when they're higher than average, competitors will shift resources to increase supply, undercut prices, and reduce profits) and the role of uncertainty in determining the demand to hold cash (since if information were costless, everyone would invest all their money and arrange it to be cashed out just at the moment that they needed to make investments, from which we can conclude that the existence of cash is a feature of a lack of information). "Perfect" competition is no guide to how to improve markets; it's a poorly chosen term for a mental model of market processes that abstracts from real world conditions of competition.

For the state to be the agency that would move markets to such "perfection," we would expect that it, too, would be the product of "perfect" democratic policies, in which infinite numbers of voters and candidates have no individual impact on policies, all policies are homogenous, and information about the costs and benefits of policies is costless. That is manifestly never the case.

The scientific method of choosing among policy options requires that choices be made from among actually available options. Both political choice and market choice are "imperfect" in all the ways specified above, so choice should be made on the basis of a comparison of real—not "perfect"—market processes and political processes.

Real markets generate a plethora of ways of providing information and generating mutually beneficial cooperation among market participants. Markets provide the framework for people to discover information, including forms of cooperation. Advertising, credit bureaus, reputation, commodity exchanges, stock exchanges, certification boards, and many other institutions arise within markets to serve the goal of facilitating mutually beneficial cooperation. Rather than discarding markets because they aren't perfect, we should look for more ways to use the market to improve the imperfect state of human welfare.

Finally, competition is better understood, not as a state of the market, but as a process of rivalrous behavior. When entrepreneurs are free to enter the market to compete with others and customers are free to choose from among producers, the rivalry among producers for the custom of customers leads to behavior favorable to those customers.

6. Markets Cannot Possibly Produce Public (Collective) Goods

If I eat an apple, you can't; consumption of an apple is purely rivalrous. If I show a movie and don't want other people to see it, I have to spend money to build walls to keep out non-payers. Some goods, those for which consumption is non-rival and exclusion is costly, cannot be produced in markets, as everyone has an incentive to wait for others to produce them. If you produce a unit, I can just consume it, so I have no incentive to produce it. The same goes for you. The publicness of such goods requires state provision, as the only means to provide them. Such goods include not only defense and provision of a legal system, but also education, transportation, health care, and many other such goods. Markets can never be relied on to produce such goods, because non-payers would free-ride off of those who pay, and since everyone would want to be a free-rider, nobody would pay. Thus, only government can produce such goods.

The public goods justification for the state is one of the most commonly misapplied of economic arguments. Whether goods are rivalrous in consumption or not is often not an inherent feature of the good, but a feature of the size of the consuming group: a swimming pool may be non-rivalrous for two people, but quite rivalrous for two hundred people. And costs of exclusion are applicable to all goods, public or private: if I want to keep you from eating my apples, I may have to take some action to protect them, such as building a fence. Many goods that are non-rivalrous in consumption, such as a professional football game (if you see it, it doesn't mean that I can't see it, too), are produced only because entrepreneurs invest in means to exclude non-payers.

Besides not being an inherent feature of the goods per se, the alleged publicness of many goods is a feature of the political decision to make the goods available on a nonexclusive and even non-priced basis. If the state produces "freeways," it's hard to see how private enterprise could produce "freeways," that is, zero-priced transportation, that could compete. But notice that the "freeway" isn't really free, since it's financed through taxes (which have a particularly harsh form of exclusion from enjoyment, known as jail), and also that the lack of pricing is the primary reason for inefficient use patterns, such as traffic jams, which reflect a lack of any mechanism to allocate scarce resources (space in traffic) to their most highly valued uses. Indeed, the trend around the world has been toward pricing of roads, which deeply undercuts the public goods argument for state provision of roads.

Many goods that are allegedly impossible to provide in markets have been, or are at present, provided through market mechanisms—from lighthouses to education to policing to transportation, which suggests that the common invocation of alleged publicness is unjustified, or at least overstated.

A common form of the argument that certain goods are allegedly only producible through state action is that there are "externalities" that are not contracted for through the price mechanism. Thus, widespread education generates public benefits beyond the benefits to the persons who are educated, allegedly justifying state provision and financing through general tax revenues. But despite the benefits to others, which may be great or small, the benefits to the persons educated are so great for them that they induce sufficient investment in education. Public benefits don't always generate the defection of free-riders. In fact, as a wealth of research is demonstrating today, when states monopolize education they often fail to produce it for the poorest of the poor, who nonetheless perceive the benefits to them of education and invest substantial percentages of their meager incomes to educate their children. Whatever externalities may be generated by their children's education does not stop them from paying their own money to procure education for their children.

Finally, it should be remembered that virtually every argument alleging the impossibility of efficient production of public goods through the market applies at least equally strongly—and in many cases much more strongly—to the likelihood that the state will produce public goods. The existence and operation of a just and law-governed state is itself a public good, that is, the consumption of its benefits is non-rivalrous (at least among the citizenry) and it would be costly to exclude non-contributors to its maintenance (such as informed voters) from the enjoyment of its benefits. The incentives for politicians and voters to produce just and efficient government are not very impressive, certainly when placed next to the incentives that entrepreneurs and consumers have to procure public goods through cooperation in the marketplace. That does not mean that the state should never have any role in producing public goods, but it should make citizens less willing to cede to the state additional responsibilities for providing goods and services. In fact, the more responsibilities are given to the state, the less likely it is to be able to produce those public goods, such as defense of the rights of its citizens from aggression, at which it might enjoy special advantages.

7. Markets Don't Work (or Are Inefficient) When There Are Negative or Positive Externalities

Markets only work when all of the effects of action are born by those who make the decisions. If people receive benefits without contributing to their production, markets will fail to produce the right amount. Similarly, if people receive "negative benefits," that is, if they are harmed and those costs are not taken into account in the decision to produce the goods, markets will benefit some at the expense of others, as the benefits of the action go to one set of parties and the costs are borne by another.

The mere existence of an externality is no argument for having the state take over some activity or displace private choices. Fashionable clothes and good grooming generate plenty of positive externalities, as others admire those who are well clothed or groomed, but that's no reason to turn choice of or provision of clothing and grooming over to the state. Gardening, architecture, and many other activities generate positive externalities on others, but people undertake to beautify their gardens and their buildings just the same. In all those cases, the benefits to the producers alone—including the approbation of those on whom the positive externalities are showered—are sufficient to induce them to produce the goods. In other cases, such as the provision of television and radio broadcasts, the public good is "tied" to the provision of other goods, such as advertising for firms; the variety of mechanisms to produce public goods is as great as the ingenuity of the entrepreneurs who produce them.

More commonly, however, it's the existence of *negative* externalities that leads people to question the efficacy or justice of market mechanisms. Pollution is the most commonly cited example. If a producer can produce products profitably because he imposes the costs of production on others who have not consented to be a part of the production process—say, by throwing huge amounts of smoke into the air or chemicals into a river—he will probably do so. Those who breathe the polluted air or drink the toxic water will bear the costs of producing the product, while the producer will get the benefits from the sale of the product. The problem in such cases, however, is not that markets have failed, but that they are absent. Markets rest on property and cannot function when property rights are not defined or enforced. Cases of pollution are precisely cases, not of market failure, but of government failure to define and defend the property rights of others, such as those who breathe polluted air or drink polluted water.

When people downwind or downstream have the right to defend their rights, they can assert their rights and stop the polluters from polluting. The producer can install at his own expense equipment or technology to eliminate the pollution (or reduce it to tolerable and non-harmful levels), or offer to pay the people downwind or downstream for the rights to use their resources (perhaps offering them a better place to live), or he must stop producing the product, because he is harming the rights of others who will not accept his offers, showing that the total costs exceed the benefits. It's property rights that make such calculations possible and that induce people to take into account the effects of their actions on others. And it's markets, that is, the opportunity to engage in free exchange of rights, that allow all of the various parties to calculate the costs of actions.

Negative externalities such as air and water pollution are not a sign of market failure, but of government's failure to define and defend the property rights on which markets rest.

8. The More Complex a Social Order Is, the Less It Can Rely on Markets and the More It Needs Government Direction

Reliance on markets worked fine when society was less complicated, but with the tremendous growth of economic and social connections, government is necessary to direct and coordinate the actions of so many people.

If anything, the opposite is true. A simple social order, such as a band of hunters or gatherers, might be coordinated effectively by a leader with the power to compel obedience. But as social relations become more complex, reliance on voluntary market exchange becomes more—not less—important. A complex social order requires the coordination of more information than any mind or group of minds could master. Markets have evolved mechanisms to transmit information in a relatively low-cost manner; prices encapsulate information about supply and demand in the form of units that are comparable among different goods and services, in ways that voluminous reports by government bureaucracies cannot. Moreover, prices translate across languages, social mores, and ethnic and religious divides and allow people to take advantage of the knowledge possessed by unknown persons thousands of miles away, with whom they will never have any other kind of relationship. The more complex an economy and society, the more important reliance on market mechanisms becomes.

9. Markets Don't Work in Developing Countries

Markets work well in countries with well developed infrastructures and legal systems, but in their absence developing countries simply cannot afford recourse to markets. In such cases, state direction is necessary, at least until a highly developed infrastructure and legal system is developed that could allow room for markets to function.

In general, infrastructure development is a feature of the wealth accumulated through markets, not a condition for markets to exist, and the failure of a legal system is a reason why markets are underdeveloped, but that failure is a powerful reason to reform the legal system so it could provide the foundation for the development of markets, not to postpone legal reform and market development. The only way to achieve the wealth of developed countries is to create the legal and institutional foundations for markets so that entrepreneurs, consumers, investors, and workers can freely cooperate to create wealth.

All currently wealthy countries were once very poor, some within living memory. What needs explanation is not poverty, which is the natural state of mankind, but wealth. Wealth has to be created and the best way to ensure that wealth is created is to generate the incentives for people to do so. No system better than the free market, based on well defined and legally secure property rights and legal institutions to facilitate exchange, has ever been discovered for generating incentives for wealth creation. There is one path out of poverty, and that is the path of wealth creation through the free market.

The term "developing nation" is frequently misapplied when it is applied to nations whose governments have rejected markets in favor of central planning, state ownership, mercantilism, protectionism, and special privileges. Such nations are not, in fact, developing at all. The nations that are developing, whether starting from relatively wealthy or relatively impoverished positions, are those that have created legal institutions of property and contract, freed markets, and limited the powers, the budget, and the reach of the state power.

10. Markets Lead to Disastrous Economic Cycles, Such as the Great Depression

Reliance on market forces leads to cycles of "boom and bust" as investor overconfidence feeds on itself, leading to massive booms in investment that are inevitably followed by contractions of production, unemployment, and a generally worsening economic condition.

Economic cycles of "boom and bust" are sometimes blamed on reliance on markets. The evidence, however, is that generalized overproduction is not a feature of markets; when more goods and services are produced, prices adjust and the result is general affluence, not a "bust." When this or that industry expands beyond the ability of the market to sustain profitability, a process

69

of self-correction sets in, and profit signals lead resources to be redirected to other fields of activity. There is no reason inherent in markets for such correction to apply to all industries; indeed, it is self-contradictory (for if investment is being taken away from all and redirected to all, then it's not being taken away from all in the first place).

Nonetheless, prolonged periods of general unemployment are possible when governments distort price systems through foolish manipulation of monetary systems, a policy error that is often combined with subsidies to industries that should be contracting and wage and price controls that keep the market from adjusting, thus prolonging the unemployment. Such was the case of the Great Depression that lasted from 1929 to the end of World War II, which economists (such as Nobel Prize winner Milton Friedman) showed was caused by a massive and sudden contraction in the money supply by the U.S. Federal Reserve system, which was pursuing politically set goals. The general contraction was then deepened by the rise in protectionism, which extended the suffering worldwide, and prolonged greatly by such programs as the National Recovery Act, programs to keep farm prices high (by destroying huge quantities of agricultural products and restricting supply), and other "New Deal" programs that were aimed at keeping market forces from correcting the disastrous effects of the government's policy errors. More recent crashes, such as the Asian financial crisis of 1997, have been caused by imprudent monetary and exchange rate policies that distorted the signals to investors. Market forces corrected the policy failures of governments, but the process was not without hardship; the cause of the hardship was not the medicine that cured the disease, but the bad monetary and exchange-rate policies of governments that caused it in the first place.

With the adoption of more prudent monetary policies by governmental monetary authorities, such cycles have tended to even out. When combined with greater reliance on market adjustment processes, the result has been a reduction in the frequency and severity of economic cycles and long-term and sustained improvement in those countries that have followed policies of freedom of trade, budgetary restraint, and the rule of law.

11. Too Much Reliance on Markets Is As Silly As Too Much Reliance on Socialism: the Best Is the Mixed Economy

Most people understand that it's unwise to put all your eggs in one basket. Prudent investors diversify their portfolios and it's just as reasonable to have a diversified "policy portfolio," as well, meaning a mix of socialism and markets.

Prudent investors who don't have inside information do indeed diversify their portfolios against risk. If one stock goes down, another may go up, thus evening out the loss with a gain. Over the long run, a properly diversified portfolio will grow. But policies aren't like that. Some have been demonstrated time and time gain to fail, while others have been demonstrated to succeed. It would make no sense to have a "diversified investment portfolio" made up of stocks in firms that are known to be failing and stocks in firms that are known to be succeeding; the reason for diversification is that one doesn't have any special knowledge of which firms are more likely to be profitable or unprofitable.

Studies of decades of economic data carried out annually by the Fraser Institute of Canada and a worldwide network of research institutes have shown consistently that greater reliance on market forces leads to higher per capita incomes, faster economic growth, lower unemployment, longer life spans, lower infant mortality, falling rates of child labor, greater access to clean water, health care, and other amenities of modern life, including cleaner environments, and improved governance, such as lower rates of official corruption and more democratic accountability. Free markets generate good results.

Moreover, there is no "well balanced" middle of the road. State interventions into the market typically lead to distortions and even crises, which then are used as excuses for yet more interventions, thus driving policy one direction or another. For example, a "policy portfolio" that included imprudent monetary policy, which increases the supply of money faster than the economy is growing, will lead to rising prices. History has shown repeatedly that politicians tend to respond, not by blaming their own imprudent policies, but by blaming an "overheated economy" or "unpatriotic speculators" and imposing controls on prices. When prices are not allowed to be corrected by supply and demand (in this case, the increased supply of money, which tends to cause the price of money, as expressed in terms of commodities, to fall), the result is shortages of goods and services, as more people seek to buy limited supplies of goods at the below-market price than producers are willing to supply at that price. In addition, the lack of free markets leads people to shift to black markets, under-the-table-bribes of officials, and other departures from the rule of law. The resulting mixture of shortage and corruption then typically induces yet greater tendencies toward authoritarian assertions of power. The effect of creating a "policy portfolio" that includes such proven bad policies is to undermine the economy, to create corruption, and even to undermine constitutional democracy.

Hybrid Ethical/Economic Criticisms

12. Markets Lead to More Inequality than Non-Market Processes

By definition, markets reward ability to satisfy consumer preferences and as abilities differ, so incomes will differ. Moreover, by definition, socialism is a state of equality, so every step toward socialism is a step toward equality.

If we want to understand the relationships between policies and outcomes, it should be kept in mind that property is a legal concept; wealth is an economic concept. The two are often confused, but they should be kept distinct. Market processes regularly redistribute wealth on a massive scale. In contrast, unwilling redistribution of property (when undertaken by individual citizens, it's known as "theft") is prohibited under the rules that govern free markets, which require that property be well defined and legally secure. Markets can redistribute wealth, even when property titles remain in the same hands. Every time the value of an asset (in which an owner has a property right) changes, the wealth of the asset owner changes. An asset that was worth 600 Euros yesterday may today be worth only 400 Euros. That's a redistribution of 200 Euros of wealth through the market, although there has been no redistribution of property. So markets regularly redistribute wealth and in the process give owners of assets incentives to maximize their value or to shift their assets to those who will. That regular redistribution, based on incentives to maximize total value, represents transfers of wealth on a scale unthinkable for most politicians. In contrast, while market processes redistribute wealth, political processes redistribute property, by taking it from some and giving it to others; in the process, by making property less secure, such redistribution tends to make property in general less valuable, that is, to destroy wealth. The more unpredictable the redistribution, the greater the loss of wealth caused by the threat of redistribution of property.

Equality is a characteristic that can be realized along a number of different dimensions, but generally not across all. For example, people can all be equal before the law, but if that is the case, it is unlikely that they will have exactly equal influence over politics, for some who exercise their equal rights to freedom of speech will be more eloquent or energetic than others, and thus more influential. Similarly, equal rights to offer goods and services on free markets may not lead to exactly equal incomes, for some may work harder or longer (because they prefer income to leisure) than others, or have special skills for which others will pay extra. On the flip side, the attempt to achieve through coercion equality of influence or equality of incomes will entail that some exercise more authority or political power than others, that is, the power necessary to bring about such outcomes. In order to bring about a particular pattern of outcomes, someone or some group must have the "God's Eye" view of outcomes necessary to redistribute, to see a lack here and a surplus there and thus to take from here and move to there. As powers to create equal outcomes are concentrated in the hands of those entrusted with them, as was the case in the officially egalitarian Soviet Union, those with unequal political and legal powers find themselves tempted to use those powers to attain unequal incomes or access to resources. Both logic and experience show that conscious attempts to attain equal or "fair" incomes, or some other pattern other than what the spontaneous order of the market generates, are generally self-defeating, for the simple reason that those who hold the power to redistribute property use it to benefit themselves, thus converting inequality of political power into other sorts of inequality, whether honors, wealth, or something else. Such was certainly the experience of the officially communist nations and such is the path currently being taken by other nations, such as Venezuela, in which total power is being accumulated in the hands of one man, Hugo Chavez, who demands such massively unequal power, ostensibly in order to create equality of wealth among citizens.

According to the data in the 2006 *Economic Freedom of the World Report*, reliance on free markets is weakly correlated to income inequality (from the least free to the most free economies the world over, divided into quartiles, the percentage of income received by the poorest ten percent varies from an average of 2.2 percent to an average of 2.5 percent), but it is very strongly correlated to the levels of income of the poorest ten percent (from the least free to the most free economies the world over, divided into quartiles, the average levels of income received by the poorest ten percent are $826, $1,186, $2,322, and $6,519). Greater reliance on markets seems to have little impact on income distributions, but it does substantially raise the incomes of the poor and it is likely that many of the poor would certainly consider that a good thing.

13. Markets Cannot Meet Human Needs, Such as Health, Housing, Education, and Food

Goods should be distributed according to principles appropriate to their nature. Markets distribute goods according to ability to pay, but health, housing, education, food, and other basic human needs, precisely because they are needs, should be distributed according to need, not ability to pay.

If markets do a better job of meeting human needs than other principles, that is, if more people enjoy higher standards of living under markets than under socialism, it seems that the allocation mechanism under markets does a better job of meeting the criterion of need, as well. As noted above, the incomes of the poorest tend to rise rapidly with the degree of market freedom, meaning that the poor have more resources with which to satisfy their needs. (Naturally, not all needs are directly related to income;

true friendship and love certainly are not. But there is no reason to think that those are more "equitably" distributed by coercive mechanisms, either, or even that they can be distributed by such mechanisms.)

Moreover, while assertions of "need" tend to be rather rubbery claims, as are assertions of "ability," willingness to pay is easier to measure. When people bid with their own money for goods and services, they are telling us how much they value those goods and services relative to other goods and services. Food, certainly a more basic need than education or health care, is provided quite effectively through markets. In fact, in those countries where private property was abolished and state allocation substituted for market allocation, the results were famine and even cannibalism. Markets meet human needs for most goods, including those that respond to basic human needs, better than do other mechanisms.

Satisfaction of needs requires the use of scarce resources, meaning that choices have to be made about their allocation. Where markets are not allowed to operate, other systems and criteria for rationing scarce resources are used, such as bureaucratic allocation, political pull, membership in a ruling party, relationship to the president or the main holders of power, or bribery and other forms of corruption. It is hardly obvious that such criteria are better than the criteria evolved by markets, nor that they generate more equality; the experience is rather the opposite.

14. Markets Rest on the Principle of the Survival of the Fittest

Just like the law of the jungle, red in tooth and claw, the law of the market means survival of the fittest. Those who cannot produce to market standards fall by the wayside and are trampled underfoot.

Invocations of evolutionary principles such as "survival of the fittest" in the study of living systems and in the study of human social interaction lead to confusion unless they identify what it is in each case that survives. In the case of biology, it is the individual animal and its ability to reproduce itself. A rabbit that is eaten by a cat because it's too slow to escape isn't going to have any more offspring. The fastest rabbits will be the ones to reproduce. When applied to social evolution, however, the unit of survival is quite different; it's not the individual human being, but the form of social interaction, such as a custom, an institution, or a firm, that is "selected" in the evolutionary struggle. When a business firm goes out of business, it "dies", that is to say, that particular form of social cooperation "dies", but that certainly doesn't mean that the human beings who made up the firm—as investors, owners, managers, employees, and so on—die, as well. A less efficient form of cooperation is replaced by a more efficient form. Market competition is decidedly unlike the competition of the jungle. In the jungle animals compete to eat each other, or to displace each other. In the market, entrepreneurs and firms compete with each other for the right to cooperate with consumers and with other entrepreneurs and firms. Market competition is not competition for the opportunity to live; it is competition for the opportunity to cooperate.

15. Markets Debase Culture and Art

Art and culture are responses to the higher elements of the human soul and, as such, cannot be bought and sold like tomatoes or shirt buttons. Leaving art to the market is like leaving religion to the market, a betrayal of the inherent dignity of art, as of religion. Moreover, as art and culture are opened more and more to competition on international markets, the result is their debasement, as traditional forms are abandoned in the pursuit of the almighty dollar or euro.

Most art has been and is produced for the market. Indeed, the history of art is largely the history of innovation through the market in response to new technologies, new philosophies, new tastes, and new forms of spirituality. Art, culture, and the market have been intimately connected for many centuries. Musicians charge fees for people to attend their concerts, just as vegetable mongers charge for tomatoes or tailors charge to replace buttons on suits. In fact, the creation of wider markets for music, film, and other forms of art by the creation of records, cassettes, CDs, DVDs, and now iTunes and mp3 files allows more and more people to be exposed to more and more varied art, and for artists to create more artistic experiences, to create more hybrid forms of art, and to earn more income. Unsurprisingly, most of the art produced in any given year won't stand the test of time; that creates a false perspective on the part of those who condemn contemporary art as "trashy," in comparison to the great works of the past; what they are comparing are the best works winnowed out from hundreds of years of production to the mass of works produced in the past year. Had they included all of the works that did not stand the test of time and were not remembered, the comparison would probably look quite different. What accounts for the survival of the best is precisely the competitive process of markets for art.

Comparing the entirety of contemporary artistic production with the very best of the best from past centuries is not the only error people make when evaluating markets for art. Another error common to observers from wealthy societies who visit poor societies is the confusion of the poverty of poor societies with their cultures. When wealthy visitors see people in countries that are poor-but-growing-economically using cell phones and flipping open laptops, they complain that their visit is not as "authentic" as the last one. As people become richer through market interactions made possible by increasing liberalization or globalization, such as the introduction of cell telephony, antiglobalization activists from rich countries complain that the poor are being "robbed" of their culture. But why equate culture with poverty? The Japanese went from poverty to wealth and it would be hard to argue that they are any less Japanese as a result. In fact, their greater wealth has made possible the spread of awareness of Japanese culture around the world. In India, as incomes are rising, the fashion industry is responding by turning to traditional forms of attire, such as the sari, and adapting, updating, and applying to it aesthetic criteria of beauty and form. The very small country of Iceland has managed to maintain a high literary culture and their own theater and movie industry because per capita incomes are quite high, allowing them to dedicate their wealth to perpetuating and developing their culture.

Finally, although religious belief is not "for sale," free societies do leave religion to the same principles—equal rights and freedom of choice—as those at the foundation of the free market. Churches, mosques, synagogues, and temples compete with each other for adherents and for support. Unsurprisingly, those European countries that provide official state support of churches tend to have very low church participation, whereas countries without state support of religion tend to have higher levels of church participation. The reason is not so hard to understand: churches that have to compete for membership and support have to provide services—sacramental, spiritual, and communal—to members, and that greater attention to the needs of the membership tends to create more religiosity and participation. Indeed, that's why the official established state church of Sweden lobbied to be disestablished in the year 2000; as an unresponsive part of the state bureaucracy, the church was losing connection with its members and potential members and was, in effect, dying.

There is no contradiction between the market and art and culture. Market exchange is not the same as artistic experience or cultural enrichment, but it is a helpful vehicle for advancing both.

16. Markets Only Benefit the Rich and Talented

The rich get richer and the poor get poorer. If you want to make a lot of money, you have to start out with a lot. In the race of the market for profits, those who start out ahead reach the finish line first.

Market processes aren't races, which have winners and losers. When two parties voluntarily agree to exchange, they do so because they both expect to benefit, not because they hope they will win and the other will lose. Unlike in a race, in an exchange, if one person wins, it doesn't mean that the other has to lose. Both parties gain. The point is not to "beat" the other, but to gain through voluntary cooperative exchange; in order to induce the other person to exchange, you have to offer a benefit to him or her, as well.

Being born to wealth may certainly be a good thing, something the citizens of wealthy countries probably do not appreciate as much as do those who seek to emigrate from poor countries to rich countries; the latter usually understand the benefits of living in a wealthy society better than those who are born to it. But within a free market, with freedom of entry and equal rights for all buyers and sellers, those who were good at meeting market demands yesterday may not be the same as those who will be good at meeting market demand tomorrow. Sociologists refer to the "circulation of elites" that characterizes free societies; rather than static elites that rest on military power, caste membership, or tribal or family connection, the elites of free societies—including artistic elites, cultural elites, scientific elites, and economic elites—are open to new members and rarely pass on membership to the children of members, many of whom move from the upper classes to the middle classes.

Wealthy societies are full of successful people who left behind countries where markets are severely restricted or hampered by special favors for the powerful, by protectionism, and by mercantilistic monopolies and controls, where opportunities for advancement in the market are limited. They left those societies with little or nothing and found success in more open and market-oriented societies, such as the USA, the United Kingdom, and Canada. What was the difference between the societies they left and those they joined?: freedom to compete in the market. How sad for poor countries it is that the mercantilism and restrictions in their home countries drive them abroad, so they can not stay at home and enrich their neighbors and friends by putting their entrepreneurial drive to work.

Generally, in countries with freer markets, the greatest fortunes are made, not by satisfying the desires of the rich, but by satisfying the desires of the more modest classes. From Ford Motors to Sony to Wal-Mart, great companies that generate great fortunes tend to be those that cater, not to the tastes of the richest, but to the lower and middle classes.

Free markets tend to be characterized by a "circulation of elites," with no one guaranteed a place or kept from entering by accident of birth. The phrase "the rich get richer and the poor get poorer" applies, not to free markets, but to mercantilism and political cronyism, that is, to systems in which proximity to power determines wealth. Under markets, the more common experience is that the rich do well (but may not stay "rich" by the standards of their society) and the poor get a lot richer, with many moving into the middle and upper classes. At any given moment, by definition 20 percent of the population will be in the lowest quintile of income and 20 percent will be in the highest quintile.

But it does not follow either that those quintiles will measure the same amount of income (as incomes of all income groups rise in expanding economies) or that the income categories will be filled by the same people. The categories are rather like rooms in a hotel or seats on a bus; they are filled by someone, but not always by the same people. When income distributions in market-oriented societies are studied over time, a great deal of income mobility is revealed, with remarkable numbers of people moving up and down in the income distributions. What is most important, however, is that prosperous market economies see all incomes rise, from the lowest to the highest.

17. When Prices Are Liberalized and Subject to Market Forces, They Just Go Up

The fact is that when prices are left to market forces, without government controls, they just go up, meaning that people can afford less and less. Free-market pricing is just another name for high prices.

Prices that are controlled at below market levels do tend to rise, at least over the short time, when they are freed. But there is much more to the story than that. For one thing, some controlled prices are kept above the market level, so that when they are freed, they tend to fall. Moreover, when looking at money prices that are controlled by state power, it's important to remember that the money that changes hands over the table is not usually the only price paid by those who successfully purchase the goods. If the goods are rationed by queuing, then the time spent waiting in line is a part of what people have to spend to get the goods. (Notably, however, that waiting time represents pure waste, since it's not time that is somehow transferred to producers to induce them to make more of the goods to satisfy the unmet demand.) If corrupt officials have their hands open, there are also the payments under the table that have to be added to the payment that is made over the table. The sum of the legal payment, the illegal bribes, and the time spent waiting in lines when maximum prices are imposed by the state on goods and services is quite often higher than the price that people would agree on through the market. Moreover, the money spent on bribes and the time spent on waiting are wasted—they are spent by consumers but not received by producers, so they provide no incentive for producers to produce more and thereby alleviate the shortage caused by price controls.

While money prices may go up in the short term when prices are freed, the result is to increase production and diminish wasteful rationing and corruption, with the result that total real prices—expressed in terms of a basic commodity, human labor time—goes down. The amount of time that a person had to spend laboring to earn a loaf of bread in 1800 was a serious fraction of his or her laboring day; as wages have gone up and up and up and up, the amount of working time necessary to buy a loaf of bread has fallen to just a few minutes in wealthy countries. Measured in terms of labor, the prices of all other goods have fallen dramatically, with one exception: labor itself. As labor productivity and wages rise, hiring human labor becomes more expensive, which is why modestly well off people in poor countries commonly have servants, whereas even very wealthy people in rich countries find it much cheaper to buy machines to wash their clothes and dishes. The result of free markets is a fall in the price of everything else in terms of labor, and a rise in the price of labor in terms of everything else.

18. Privatization and Marketization in Post-Communist Societies Were Corrupt, Which Shows that Markets Are Corrupting

Privatization campaigns are almost always rigged. It's a game that just awards the best state assets to the most ruthless and corrupt opportunists. The whole game of privatization and marketization is dirty and represents nothing more than theft from the people.

A variety of formerly socialist states that have created privatization campaigns have had quite varied outcomes. Some have generated very successful market orders. Others have slipped back toward authoritarianism and have seen the "privatization" processes result in new elites gaining control of both the state and private businesses, as in the emerging "Siloviki" system of Russia. The dirtiness of the dirty hands that profited from rigged privatization schemes was a result of the preexisting lack of market institutions, notably the rule of law that is the foundation for the market. Creating those institutions is no easy task and there is no well-known generally applicable technique that works in all cases. But the failure in some cases to fully realize the institutions of the rule of law is no reason not to try; even in the case of Russia, the deeply flawed privatization schemes that were instituted were an improvement over the one-party tyranny that preceded them and that collapsed from its own injustice and inefficiency.

Mere "privatization" in the absence of a functioning legal system is not the same as creating a market. Markets rest on a foundation of law; failed privatizations are not failures of the market, but failures of the state to create the legal foundations for markets.

OVERLY ENTHUSIASTIC DEFENSES

19. All Relations Among Humans Can Be Reduced to Market Relations

All actions are taken because the actors are maximizing their own utility. Even helping other people is getting a benefit for yourself, or you wouldn't do it. Friendship and love represent exchanges of services for mutual benefit, no less than exchanges involving sacks of potatoes. Moreover, all forms of human interaction can be understood in terms of markets, including politics, in which votes are exchanged for promises of benefits, and even crime, in which criminals and victims exchange, in the well-known example, "your money or your life."

Attempting to reduce all actions to a single motivation falsifies human experience. Parents don't think about the benefits to themselves when they sacrifice for their children or rush to their rescue when they're in danger. When people pray for salvation or spiritual enlightenment, their motivations are not quite the same as when they are shopping for clothes. What they do have in common is that their actions are purposeful, that they are undertaken to achieve their purposes. But it does not follow logically from that that the purposes they are striving to achieve are all reducible to commensurable units of the same substance. Our purposes and motivations may be varied; when we go to the market to buy a hammer, when we enter an art museum, and when we cradle a newborn baby, we are realizing very different purposes, not all of which are well expressed in terms of buying and selling in markets.

It is true that intellectual constructs and tools can be used to understand and illuminate a variety of different kinds of interaction. The concepts of economics, for example, which are used to understand exchanges on markets, can also be used to understand political science and even religion. Political choices may have calculable costs and benefits, just like business choices; political parties or mafia cartels may be compared to firms in the market. But it does not follow from such applications of concepts that the two choice situations are morally or legally equivalent. A criminal who offers you a choice between keeping your money and keeping your life is not relevantly like an entrepreneur who offers you a choice between keeping your money and using it to buy a commodity, for the simple reason that the criminal forces you to choose between two things to both of which you have a moral and legal entitlement, whereas the entrepreneur offers you a choice between two things, to one of which he has an entitlement and to one of which you have an entitlement. In both cases you make a choice and act purposively, but in the former case the criminal has forced you to choose, whereas in the latter case the entrepreneur has offered you a choice; the former lessens your entitlements and the latter offers to increase them, by offering you something you don't have but may value more for something you do have but may value less. Not all human relationships are reducible to the same terms as markets; at the very least, those that involve involuntary "exchanges" are radically different, because they represent losses of opportunity and value, rather than opportunities to gain value.

20. Markets Can Solve All Problems without Government at All

Government is so incompetent that it can't do anything right. The main lesson of the market is that we should always weaken government, because government is simply the opposite of the market. The less government you have, the more market you have.

Those who recognize the benefits of markets should recognize that in much of the world, perhaps all of it, the basic problem is not only that governments do too much, but also that they do too little. The former category—things that governments should not do, includes A) activities that should not be done by anyone at all, such as "ethnic cleansing," theft of land, and creating special legal privileges for elites, and B) things that could and should be done through the voluntary interaction of firms and entrepreneurs in markets, such as manufacturing automobiles, publishing newspapers, and running restaurants. Governments should stop doing all of those things. But as they cease doing what they ought not to do, governments should start doing some of the things that would in fact increase justice and create the foundation for voluntary inter-action to solve problems. In fact, there is a relation between the two: governments that spend their resources running car factories or publishing newspapers—or worse, confiscating property and creating legal privileges for the few—both undercut and diminish their abilities to provide truly valuable services that governments are able to provide. For example, governments in poorer nations rarely do a good job of providing clear legal title, not to mention securing property from takings. Legal systems are frequently inefficient, cumbersome, and lack the independence and impartiality that are necessary to facilitate voluntary transactions.

For markets to be able to provide the framework for social coordination, property and contract must be well established in law. Governments that fail to provide those public benefits keep markets from emerging. Government can serve the public interest by exercising authority to create law and justice, not by being weak, but by being legally authoritative and at the same time limited in its powers. A weak government is not the same as a limited government. Weak unlimited governments can be tremendously dangerous because they do things that ought not to be done but do not have the authority to enforce the rules of just conduct and provide the security of life, liberty, and estate that are necessary for freedom and free market exchanges. Free markets are not the same as the sheer absence of government. Not all anarchies are attractive, after all. Free markets are made possible by efficiently administered limited governments that clearly define and impartially enforce rules of just conduct.

It is also important to remember that there are plenty of

problems that have to be solved through conscious action; it's not enough to insist that impersonal market processes will solve all problems. In fact, as Nobel Prize winning economist Ronald Coase explained in his important work on the market and the firm, firms typically rely on conscious planning and coordination to achieve common aims, rather than on constant recourse to market exchanges, because going to the market is costly. Each contract arranged is costly to negotiate, for example, so long-term contracts are used instead to reduce contracting costs. In firms, long-term contracts substitute for spot-exchanges and include labor relations involving teamwork and conscious direction, rather than constant bidding for particular services. Firms—little islands of teamwork and planning—are able to succeed because they navigate within a wider ocean of spontaneous order through market exchanges. (The great error of the socialists was to try to manage the entire economy like one great firm; it would be a similar error not to recognize the limited role of conscious direction and teamwork within the wider spontaneous order of the market.) To the extent that markets can provide the framework of creation and enforcement of rules of just conduct, advocates of free markets should promote just that. Private security firms are often better than state police (and less violent, if for no other reason than that the costs of violence are not easily shifted to third parties, except by the state); voluntary arbitration often works far better than state courts. But recognizing that entails recognizing the central role of rules in creating markets and thus favoring efficient and just rules, whether provided by government or by the market, rather than merely being "antigovernment."

Finally, it should be remembered that property and market exchange may not, by themselves, solve all problems. For example, if global warming is in fact a threat to the entire planet's ability to sustain life, or if the ozone layer is being degraded in ways that will be harmful to life, coordinated government solutions may be the best, or perhaps the only, way to avoid disaster. Naturally, that does not mean that markets would play no role at all; markets for rights to carbon dioxide emissions might, for example, help to smooth adjustments, but those markets would first have to be established by coordination among governments. What is important to remember, however, is that deciding that a tool is not adequate and appropriate for all conceivable problems does not entail that it is not adequate and appropriate for any problems. The tool may work very well for some or even most problems. Property and markets solve many problems and should be relied on to do so; if they do not solve all, that is no reason to reject them for problems for which they do offer efficient and just solutions.

Free markets may not solve every conceivable problem humanity might face, but they can and do produce freedom and prosperity, and there is something to be said for that.

The Bastiat's Legacy Essay Contest

1 Grand Prize: $1,000
+ *Scholarship to 2010 International Students For Liberty Conference*

1 Second Place Prize: $200
+ *Scholarship to 2010 International Students For Liberty Conference*

8 Runners Up: $100 each

Essay Topic:
Relate the central theme in one of Bastiat's essays to a current public policy issue.

Registration Deadline December 1, 2010

Learn more at

www.StudentsForLiberty.org

Beat Back Socialism: Now Is the Time!

The Atlas Economic Research Foundation has partnered with Students for Liberty to bring you *The Economics of Freedom: What Your Professors Won't Tell You* and the associated essay contest. It's a part of Atlas's global effort to promote sound thinking about public policy and liberty.

Atlas's Property Not Plunder: The Bastiat Legacy program involves teams around the globe working in fourteen languages to combat statism, violence, plunder, and war.

Find out more at www.AtlasNetwork.org

- The Atlas Network spans over 80 countries and includes more than 200 organizations dedicated to liberty.

- Atlas organizes training seminars, regional conferences, and many other programs to empower Intellectual Entrepreneurs who believe in liberty.

- Atlas maintains an online "Think Tank Toolkit," an interactive Network Directory, and a Global Events Calendar.

ATLAS

ECONOMIC RESEARCH FOUNDATION

Our Friends Are Working for Liberty. Are You?
Sponsor the Atlas Network for Freedom!

SUDAN

Durra Elmaki
*Nile Institue for
Economic Studies*

MOZAMBIQUE

Manuel d'Araujo
*Center for Mozambican
and International Studies*

USA

Jamie Story
*Grassroots Institute
of Hawaii*

KYRGYZSTAN

Mirsulzhan Namazaliev
*Central Asian Free-
Market Institute*

MEXICO

Odile Mauri
*Liberal Network
for Latin America*

The Atlas Economic Research Foundation is a non-profit organization that connects organizations and individuals with ideas and each other to promote liberty. Atlas accepts no government funding. Atlas relies upon voluntary contributions from individuals who want to spread the ideas of liberty in the U.S. and worldwide.

Get involved
www.atlasnetwork.org

Students For Liberty

A Free Academy, A Free Society

Students For Liberty is a network of pro-liberty students all over the world. We work to educate our fellow students on the ideas of individual, economic, and academic freedom.

Students For Liberty can help you with:

- Leadership training
- Tips on how to start a student group
- Finding speakers to host on campus
- Obtaining free books for a reading club
- Student Conferences

www.StudentsForLiberty.org

Students For Liberty
Conferences

Do you want to:

- Learn about the philosophy of liberty?
- Meet fellow students and leaders of liberty?
- Receive training on how to best advance liberty?

Then join us for the

2010 Fall Regional Conferences

- Boston, MA
- New York City, NY
- Philadelphia, PA
- Atlanta, GA
- Chicago, IL
- Austin, TX
- Phoenix, AZ
- Los Angeles, CA
- San Francisco, CA

2011 International Students For Liberty Conference

The world's largest gathering of pro-liberty students
February 18–20, 2011
George Washington University, Washington DC

www.PoliticalConferences.org

Additional Resources for Liberty

The Foundation for Economic Education

- www.FEE.org -
- www.TheFreemanOnline.org -

The Cato Institute

- www.Cato.org -
- www.CatoOnCampus.org -

The Institute for Humane Studies

- www.TheIHS.org -

The Foundation for Individual Rights in Education

- www.TheFire.org -

The Charles G. Koch Charitable Foundation

- www.CGKFoundation.org -